atlanta

ATLANTA HISTORY CENTER

ATLANTA

APA PUBLICATIONS

Birth Home
Of
Martin L. King, Jr.

501 Auburn
Birth Home of Martin Luther King, Jr.

NATIONAL PARK SERVICE
Department of the Interior

Tours of the Birth
Home Begin Every
Half-Hour At
Visitor Information
Station
← 522 Auburn Ave., N.E.

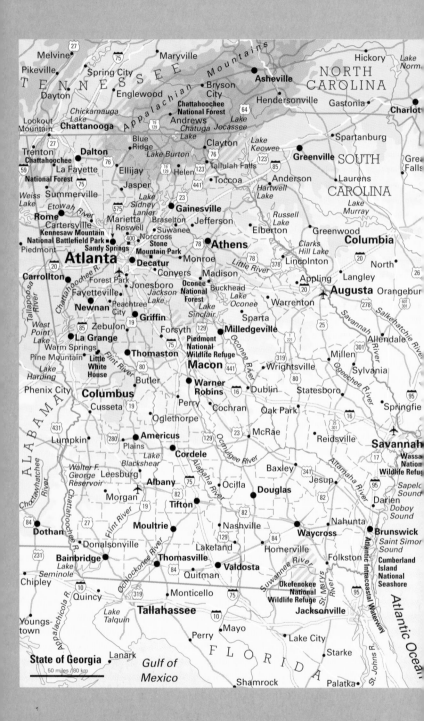

Dear Visitor!

CNN, The World of Coca-Cola, Martin Luther King, Jr, soaring skyscrapers and sweeping plantations. This is Atlanta, home of the 1996 Olympic Games. Whether this is your first visit or your one hundredth, you'll discover a city that has undergone a long-awaited renaissance, rising from the ashes of the Civil War to become the capital of the 'New South'.

In these pages Insight's correspondent will help enrich your experience of the city, turning her eye for the scenic and the savvy, the historic and the contemporary, on Atlanta's sights, streets and attractions.

 Elizabeth Boleman-Herring is a writer with Atlanta in her blood. Atlanta was where her grandfather, born in Reed Creek, Georgia in 1883, went to buy his first automobile; where her Great Uncle Bob and his friend WC used to go to trade mules, and where her Aunt Inez, age 85, was taken at the age of nine by passenger train from Seneca, South Carolina, to visit the Ostrich Farm. As an English major at the University of Georgia in Athens she visited Underground Atlanta in its second incarnation, wandered around Piedmont Park taking pictures, and fretted about Lester Maddox. Spells in Europe and writing books on Greece occupied Boleman-Herring's time until recently, when she moved back home, swiveled her green eye shade, dusted off considerable amounts of Southern charm, and got Georgia on her mind again.

We hope Boleman-Herring's first-hand knowledge of the city will help you enjoy tasting, seeing and experiencing the essence of Atlanta.

Hans Höfer
Publisher, Insight Guides

C O N T E N T S

Pages 2/3:
Fit for a King

marta

Lenox
Transit
Station

Excursions

Pages 10/11:
Pretty as a peach

Shopping, Eating Out & Nightlife

Calendar of Events

Practical Information

Maps

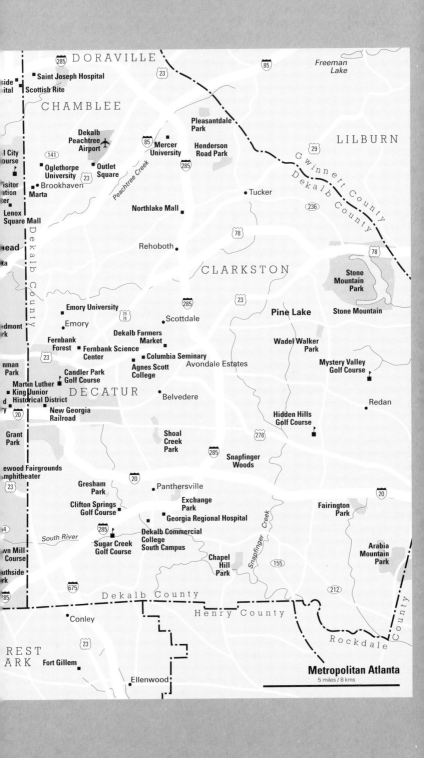

DORAVILLE

CHAMBLEE

Saint Joseph Hospital

Scottish Rite

Freeman
Lake

LILBURN

Dekalb
Peachtree
Airport

Mercer
University

Pleasantdale
Park

Henderson
Road Park

Oglethorpe
University

Outlet
Square

Brookhaven

Marta

Gwinnett County
Dekalb County

Tucker

Northlake Mall

Lenox
Square Mall

Peachtree Creek

Rehoboth

CLARKSTON

Stone
Mountain
Park

Stone Mountain

Emory University

Emory

Scottdale

Pine Lake

Dekalb County

Dekalb Farmers
Market

Wadel Walker
Park

Fernbank
Forest

Fernbank Science
Center

Columbia Seminary

Avondale Estates

Mystery Valley
Golf Course

Candler Park
Golf Course

Agnes Scott
College

Martin Luther
King Junior
Historical District

DECATUR

Belvedere

Redan

New Georgia
Railroad

Grant
Park

Hidden Hills
Golf Course

ewood Fairgrounds
mphitheater

Shoal
Creek
Park

Snapfinger
Woods

Gresham
Park

Panthersville

Exchange
Park

Clifton Springs
Golf Course

Georgia Regional Hospital

Fairington
Park

South River

Dekalb Commercial
College
South Campus

Sugar Creek
Golf Course

Snapfinger Creek

Arabia
Mountain
Park

wn Mill
Course

uthside
rk

Chapel
Hill
Park

Dekalb County

Conley

Henry County

Rockdale County

REST
ARK

Fort Gillem

Metropolitan Atlanta

5 miles / 8 kms

Ellenwood

HISTORY &

Atlantans Before Atlanta

Before the historical tribes and Indian Nations, the area around Stone Mountain and the shallow ford of the Chattahoochee River, near today's Roswell, was already a nexus of trade, communication and war routes for north Georgia's indigenous peoples. At the time of Hernando DeSoto's pioneering expedition to the Mississippi, 1540–1, there were Siouxan-speaking peoples living in coastal South Carolina, Muskogeans or Creeks (so named by the Europeans due to their propensity for settling near water) in central Georgia, and primarily Cherokees in north and north-west Georgia. The prehistoric community known as the Etowah, who flourished at a site north-west of present-day Atlanta between AD1000 and 1500, may have been linked, as part of a unified 'Southern Cult,' to the indigenous culture of Mexico.

Etowah mounds

Today, at the Etowah Indian Mounds State Historic Site, visitors may view the artifacts, earthworks and cult burials of this sophisticated people. On the banks of the Etowah River, where these early Americans fished for gar, drumfish and catfish, and turtles, for which they had a consuming passion, their 52-acre village and temple complex was encircled by a defensive moat further fortified by a 12ft-tall palisade bristling with towers. The houses within the fortress, effectively protected from aggressors bearing clubs and spears, fanned out to prevent the likelihood of village-wide fires started by fire-arrows. A packed, red-clay plaza, or prototypical town square, was overlooked by temple and burial platform mounds.

Culture

Ancestors of Creeks and Cherokees

The great temple mound, the height of a six-story building, still provides a commanding view of the fertile alluvial valley which supported life here for centuries before the Europeans came. Mound C, to the north, has yielded up the Etowah's richest artifacts: 350 burials, which have served as an archeological textbook on the so-called Mississippian Culture. In the oldest, deepest strata were found the most significant objects: two large, marble figures, male and female, each standing 2ft high and weighing about 125lbs apiece. The woman kneels, dressed in a belted skirt and discoid headdress, a 'knapsack' on her back; the male figure is seated cross-legged, a coil or chignon on the back of his head. Both figures are painted, in the manner of the ancient Greeks; and both are finely carved and polished.

The Etowah were the ancestors of warring neighbors, the Creeks and Cherokees, for whom the Chattahoochee River was to serve as a buffer. When Captain Juan Pardo arrived in north-west Georgia in 1567, sent by Spain to ring the region with forts, he became the first European to lay eyes on another site important to these Native Americans: Stone Mountain. Pardo claimed, to his death, that the 'Crystal Mountain' was strewn about with diamonds, rubies and gemstones, there for the taking, but he never succeeded in mounting a return expedition. When Colonel Marinus Willet arrived in June 1790, as part of an embassy from President George Washington, he met with tribal chieftains of the Creek Nation, and ascended to the summit of 'the southern Gibraltar.' At that time a vast, prehistoric wall crowned the monolith, and Willet noted that the inhabitants of the surrounding regions seemed a very happy people.

Etowah sculpture

The Southern Gibraltar, Stone Mountain

Inventor and novelist/cleric Francis R Goulding, who passed through in 1822, guided by a Cherokee named Kanook and accompanied by a slave boy named Scipio, preserved perhaps the most tantalizing picture of 'Atlanta before Atlanta.' He described Stone Mountain's 'remarkable wall' as 'about breast high... continuous all around the summit' with the only place of entrance 'a natural doorway under a large rock, so narrow and so low that only one man could enter at a time.'

The view from the promontory was sublime: a vast basin of virgin woodlands 'which rose on all sides to meet the blue of the sky.' In addition, atop the rock, was an immense, flat boulder measuring some 200ft in diameter, and some 5–10ft thick. This stone, destroyed by quarrymen in 1896 and known to the Europeans as The Devil's Crossroads, was split by precise, perpendicular, 4ft-wide clefts; each axis running due north/south and east/west. The entire 'compass' was surmounted by yet another flat stone which measured some 20ft across. Whatever the origins of this device, it stood atop a natural landmark used for centuries as a sort of navigational touchstone for Indian warriors and hunters plying their way between today's Columbus, Georgia and Chattanooga, Tennessee.

It was Stone Mountain, the Indian village of Standing Peachtree (probably a linguistic corruption of 'pitch' or 'resinous' tree) and the nearby shallow ford at Roswell that drew the first Caucasians to this great aboriginal crossroads in north Georgia, and the place names of even the 20th-century metropolis reflect the city's origins as a frontier town built on the ruins of the Native American culture eradicated to make way for it.

From Standing Peachtree to Terminus

By 1833–39, when South Carolinian Hardy Ivy, his wife and five children arrived to buy and settle a parcel of land that comprised all of today's downtown Atlanta – 202½ acres for $225 – the turtle-eating Etowah were long gone. Their descendants, the Creeks, had signed over all their Georgia holdings in the cessions of 1733–1826, and the Cherokee had been cruelly removed from the region, by forced march, to Indian Territory in the west: some 15,000 set out on the 'Trail of Tears,' and 4,000 perished, of disease and exposure, along the way.

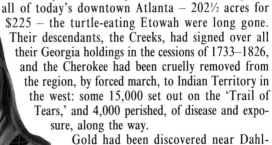

Gold had been discovered near Dahlonega, the railroad men had set their sights on north Georgia, and even the oratory of the tribe's well-educated lobbyists, many of them Christians, mostly wealthy and well-settled by the early 19th century, could not sway the bureaucrats of

Creek Indian chief

Washington. Atlanta, dates its birth from a railroad spike driven into the Cherokee heart, but if Standing Peachtree had served as a Creek and Cherokee crossroads for the purposes of commerce, conquest and communication, it was to go on as it had begun. The velocity, however, would increase dramatically.

A New Hampshire-born army engineer, Stephen H Long, was responsible for determining the placement of Atlanta's oldest urban landmark, the Zero Milepost, which still stands in downtown Atlanta (though at a site somewhat removed from its original location) in the lobby of the New Georgia Railroad depot. In a sense, it was a bench mark that became a metropolis. Driven into the ground by Abbott Hill Brisbane, Long's South Carolinian assistant, the simple stone marker designated the spot selected, for purely topographical reasons, for the southern terminus of the proposed Western & Atlantic Railroad.

In the fall of 1837, 'Terminus' was located 8 miles from Montgomery's Ferry on the Chattahoochee River, and the engineer lived long enough to see it metamorphose first into Marthasville, a provincial town named for Governor Lumpkin's daughter, then into Atlanta (a name coined from 'Atlantic' by chief railroad engineer Edgar Thomson, who felt the city was destined to become much more than a 'ville'). In the 1840s, however, the staunch West Point professor Long might have been forgiven for seeing little future for a town where cock-fighting, groggeries, gambling dens

General John Bell Hood

and brothels infested such 'suburbs' as Murrel's Row and Snake Nation. Atlanta started out as a town for toughs which educators and men of the cloth had an uphill battle to tame.

In the Wake of Sherman

In fact, Long lived just two days past the fall of the city to General William Tecumseh Sherman during the American Civil War (1861–65). Atlanta was defended by the Confederate General John Bell Hood, a 33-year-old Kentuckian with a mangled arm and a missing leg. Hood struck out at Sherman three times – in the northern part of the city at Peachtree Creek; in the Battle of Atlanta west of Decatur; and again at Ezra Church. But to no avail. The city, heavily fortified, was under siege for a month. When Confederate supplies ran out, the Union army moved in, looting and setting fire to everything in sight. In Sherman's wake, Atlanta was left smoldering, with $1.64 in the municipal coffers, and only 400 structures left standing throughout the city. Notable among these are five churches, preserved through the efforts of Father Thomas O'Reilly, pastor of the Church of the Immaculate Conception.

The Monroe Embankment and the Zero Milepost are all that remain of the earliest downtown structures. Sherman razed the rest. Even the early 19th-century storefronts lining the streets of Underground Atlanta and the Georgia Railroad Freight Depot date from the post-war period, when railroads and railroad men controlled Atlanta's destiny.

In the post-war period, however, it was in ruined Atlanta that Major General John Pope was headquartered, rather than the state capital at Milledgeville, and along with creating a new state constitution palatable to Washington, delegates to the Atlanta-based constitutional convention lobbied for moving the seat of state government to Atlanta, a proposal approved in 1868. This was the time of the so-called 'scalawags,' local whites who supported 'Yankee' policies for power and profit; of 'carpet baggers,' northern entrepreneurs who headed south for the spoils; and of the Ku Klux Klan, whose masked vigilantes actively intimidated African-American voters. Georgia's first post-war governor, Rufus B Bulloch of New York, a carpet bagger who rode in on a Republican ticket, was elected, due to the disenfranchisement of so many Georgians who had been Confederate supporters.

Confederate bitterness notwithstanding, the September 2, 1885 cornerstone ceremonies for the elegant new state Capitol were only slightly dampened by the fact that the building was constructed of Indiana limestone and built by Ohio contractors. In 20 years, Atlanta would be on its feet again, a booming state capital. But it would also remain a city deeply divided over the issue of race.

The burning of Atlanta from 'Gone with the Wind'

Expos, Oratory and Boosters

With the International Cotton Exposition of 1881, municipal boosterism became Atlanta's most enduring trait, and the city has ever since maintained its penchant for the big, self-promoting idea at the right time. The Exposition, which cost Atlanta $200,000, featured 'one-day suits' for the state governors: fashioned from cotton picked, spun into thread, dyed and tailored in Georgia, all within 24 hours, the suits and the Expo were a roaring success.

Lindbergh visits Atlanta, 1927

The Atlanta area's first international fair drew about 200,000 visitors a month. That its planner, Hannibal I Kimball, was a carpet bagger from Maine and one of the speakers was William T Sherman did not seem to matter much to Atlantans. By 1886, even Henry Woodfin Grady, prestigious editor of the *Atlanta Constitution*, was willing to close the door on the city's Confederate past. In a famous speech delivered to members of the New England Society of New York, with Sherman again in attendance, Grady spoke of the 'New South.' He chided the general for having been 'kind of careless about fire' but went on: 'from the ashes he left us...we have raised a brave and beautiful city.'

Near the turn of the century more than 100 passenger trains served Atlanta every 24 hours. Jacobs Pharmacy was dispensing chemist John S Pemberton's headache remedy, Coca-Cola, and, in 1901, the first horseless carriage arrived in town. The advent of the automobile and the airplane, the latter in 1930, marked a long decline in railway passenger service in and out of Atlanta. During the late 1920s the so-called railway gulch in the midst of downtown was eliminated by viaducts, and the nucleus of 'Underground Atlanta' came into being. Atlanta's first airport, originally an auto race track, eight miles south of downtown, got underway.

Another of Atlanta's visionary boosters, alderman, later mayor, William B Hartsfield, saw the bright future for aviation and successfully won for his home town a federal contract for the US Postal Service's New York–Miami stopover. The colorful Mr Hartsfield loved politics, his city and its people. He persuaded Charles A Lindbergh to visit Atlanta in 1927, a publicity stunt that edged out the rival city, Birmingham, Alabama, in the race to become the southern mail hub. He then cajoled the city fathers, in 1929, into purchasing Candler Field, the former auto race track. In 1971 the municipal airport was named William B Hartsfield International – now one of the busiest in the nation: Zoo Atlanta's most famous resident, the silverbacked gorilla who, along with his trio of wives, displays a fondness for television, and has already been named 'Willie B'.

Atlanta Rises Again

Today, Atlanta's Hartsfield vies with Chicago's O'Hare for the ranking of America's busiest airport: as of 1992, it was placed sixth busiest in the world, with the world's largest passenger terminal complex. Two hours of air time away from over 80 percent of the nation's population, Hartsfield offers non-stop service to 150 cities in the United States – a far cry from the handful of monoplanes originally piloted by Candler Field daredevils in 1909.

Downtown Atlanta

In fact, Atlanta has always been gifted with prescient native daughters and sons, and adopted visionaries as well. The roster of brash, successful risk-takers who have loved Atlanta stretches from former slave Alonzo Herndon, founder of the country's first African-American insurance company, the Atlanta Mutual Insurance Association, and Henry W Grady, spokesman for a New South dependent on northern investment, to Dr Martin Luther King Jr, the youngest-ever recipient of the Nobel Prize for Peace and Mayor Andrew Young, who committed $125 million in city funds to creating an entertainment complex in Underground Atlanta. From the Zero Milepost to John Portman and Associates' Westin Peachtree Plaza, the country's tallest hotel – sited where Georgia's first governor's mansion once stood – Atlanta's projects have been breathtaking in their daring. Still, in this city which preserves its early heritage of boosterism and toughness beneath a southern veneer, business has always been king and money, accompanied by charitable works, makes the man.

But one of Atlanta's epithets – 'the city too busy to hate' – is a label only recently beginning to ring true. Segregated according to race for over a century and a half, Atlanta has always been a city whose African-Americans have found themselves a city within a city, and a city beneath a city, despite the recent elections of the first African-American mayors. Henry Grady, who in 1886 assured his northern audience that in the New South 'the free negro counts more than he did as a slave,' gave voice to wishful thinking that it would take many long decades to realize as fact.

When Mayor Maynard H Jackson accepted the Olympic flag, on behalf of Atlanta, from Mayor Pasqual Maragall of Barcelona in the summer of 1992, the Georgia capital built on Cherokee land, largely with the labor first of slaves, then of under-paid African-Americans, at last came into its own as an international metropolis.

Racing towards the finish

Historical Highlights

1814 Fort Gilmer is erected at Standing Peachtree, an indigenous Indian village.

1833 Hardy Ivy is the first Caucasian settler in what is today downtown Atlanta.

1837 The area of Atlanta is selected as the 'terminus' for the Western and Atlantic Railroad.

April 6 1838 General Winfield Scott is sent to clear the region of the Cherokee; their forced march west becomes known as the 'Trail of Tears.'

1843 The hamlet of Terminus is renamed Marthasville.

1845 Marthasville is rechristened Atlanta.

1847 Atlanta is incorporated as a city.

1850 The Zero Mile Post is erected at the precise mid-point of the new city.

1852 The Atlanta and West Point Railroad is completed to Atlanta.

1864 On May 8, General William Tecumseh Sherman launches the Atlanta Campaign; on September 2, the city surrenders, and is burned to the ground on November 14.

1865 The Civil War ends.

1868 Atlanta replaces Milledgeville as Georgia's capital.

June 16 1868 First edition of the *Atlanta Constitution* is published.

1886 Henry Grady's 'New South' speech in New York City invites reconciliation. Coca-Cola goes on sale at Jacobs' Pharmacy as a headache remedy.

1892 The Coca-Cola Company is founded by Asa Candler; Joel Hurt's Equitable Building, Atlanta's first 'skyscraper,' opens.

1895 The Cotton States and International Exposition is held in Piedmont Park, and 400,000 attend; Booker T Washington delivers his 'Atlanta Compromise' speech.

1917 A catastrophic fire leaves 10,000 homeless.

1928 Viaducts raise the city center one story above ground level.

January 15 1929 Dr Martin Luther King Jr is born on Auburn Avenue.

1930 Bobby Jones, of Atlanta, wins a 'grand slam' in golf. Delta Air Lines initiates scheduled passenger service from Atlanta.

1936 Margaret Mitchell's *Gone With the Wind* is published, and one million copies sell by the month of December.

December 15 1939 *Gone With the Wind* makes its movie premiere at Loew's Grand Theatre.

1941 Delta's headquarters is moved to Atlanta.

1948 WSB-TV becomes the city's first TV station.

1952 The city incorporates surrounding areas, increasing its population from 330,000 to 430,000; its size, from 37 to 118 sq miles.

1959 Ralph McGill, editor of the *Atlanta Constitution*, is awarded a Pulitzer Prize. Lenox Square, Atlanta's first regional 'shopping center,' opens.

1961 Segregationist Lester Maddox is defeated by Ivan Allen Jr in the mayoral race; Atlanta's public schools initiate desegregation.

1963 Mayor Allen speaks in Washington, DC in support of a Civil Rights Act.

1964 Dr Martin Luther King Jr is awarded the Nobel Prize for Peace.

1965 The Braves baseball team moves from Milwaukee to Atlanta.

1968 Dr Martin Luther King Jr is assassinated in Memphis, Tennessee; the funeral is held in Atlanta.

1973 Maynard H Jackson becomes Atlanta's first African-American mayor.

1976 Opening of the Georgia World Congress Center.

1981 Andrew J Young is elected mayor, then named US Ambassador to the UN.

1990 Atlanta wins its bid to host the 26th Olympiad in the summer of 1996, the centennial of the Modern Olympics.

1994 28th Super Bowl is held at the Georgia Dome.

Day itine

The Buckhead Community, comprising the Lenox Square area and the original Buckhead region, its nexus formed by Piedmont and Roswell roads and Peachtree Road NE, will be your 'home base' for the purposes of *Insight Pocket Guide*: *Atlanta* and the following itineraries.

It is my recommendation that visitors arriving for a short stay in the city take advantage of the excellent accommodation available in Buckhead. There is a wealth of shopping and nightlife in this area plus the convenience of being located close to midtown and downtown Atlanta, major expressways and rapid transport (MARTA) stations, but you will still be able to savor the greenness of a state capital which is, after all, the sum of its beautiful, tree-rich neighborhoods.

Most of these itineraries depend on traveling by rental car, MARTA, hotel shuttle bus, or a combination of all three modes of transport. Visitors from abroad may find Atlantans' utter dependence on the private car an inexplicable cultural anomaly, but as the city is set up for people arriving with their vehicles, my directions will take rental cars into account, providing information on other forms of transport when practicable.

Greetings from Atlanta

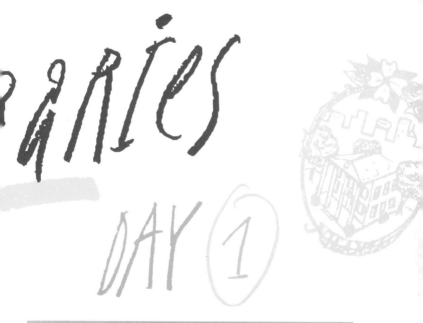

The Tullie Smith House to The World of Coca-Cola

Breakfast at Phipps Plaza; tour the Swan House, the Tullie Smith House and the Atlanta History Center; by MARTA (Lenox NE7 station to Five Points station) downtown to The World of Coca-Cola and Underground Atlanta for shopping and snacking; dinner at Anthony's.

As far in advance as possible, and by fax from abroad, reserve a table for dinner at **Anthony's** (tel: 404-262-7379; fax: 404-261-6009). I have chosen Anthony's for its splendid cuisine and genuine Southern charm, but if it is booked solid, three other venues are highly recommended: **Danté's Down the Hatch**, for dinner plus jazz, in Buckhead, but with a second location in Underground Atlanta; the **Buckhead Diner**, for 'uppity' nouveau-southern fare; and, at the Hotel Nikko, **Kamogawa**, complete with *tatami* room, Atlanta's outstanding Asian

restaurant. (See *Eating Out* for details and an annotated list of Atlanta's best restaurants.) In addition, consult your concierge or phone 404-261-1837 to learn the starting time of the first **Atlanta History Center** Tullie Smith House tour.

If you are getting an early start, begin with a cream cheese-topped bagel or fresh muffin at **Jerry Sachs's My Favorite Muffin** (Monday to Thursday 7.30am–9pm, Friday and Saturday 7.30am–11pm, Sunday 10am–6pm). Located on Level M3 of the **Phipps Plaza** shopping mall (3500 Peachtree Road NE), it features 30 different varieties of muffins, including fat-free and sugar-free, flavored coffees, herbal teas, freshly squeezed orange juice and a full espresso bar. Downstairs, on Level M1, across from Abercrombie & Fitch, is **Il centro** (Monday to Thursday 9.30am–9pm, Friday 9.30am–10pm, Saturday 9.30am–10.30pm), a European coffee bar for those getting a late start and who are interested in *lattes* (iced or hot), scones, waffle cookies and shortbread. (The Canella coffee, both the eye-opening variety and the Swiss water-process decaffeinated, is especially good.)

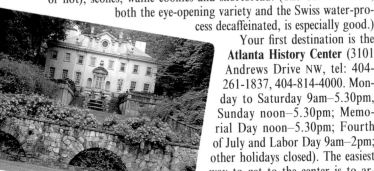

The Swan House

Your first destination is the **Atlanta History Center** (3101 Andrews Drive NW, tel: 404-261-1837, 404-814-4000. Monday to Saturday 9am–5.30pm, Sunday noon–5.30pm; Memorial Day noon–5.30pm; Fourth of July and Labor Day 9am–2pm; other holidays closed). The easiest way to get to the center is to arrange for your hotel shuttle bus to drop you off and then phone the hotel to be collected when you have completed your visit.

Your reasonably priced admission ticket admits you to all exhibits at the **Museum of Atlanta History**, two historic house tours, and the gardens and grounds of this 32-acre site. If you have time before your first house tour sets out, browse in the museum shop for books of local interest, cards and souvenirs.

The **Tullie Smith House**, built by cotton planter Robert Hiram Smith, an authentic 1830s farmhouse with freestanding open-hearth kitchen and smokehouse, working barn, farm outbuildings and herb garden, provides an historically accurate picture of rural antebellum life near Atlanta. The guided tour of this 'plantation plain style' house answers such questions as why unmarried daughters in the Old South were called spinsters, where Americans picked up such perplexing phrases as 'pop goes the weasel,' 'pot liquor' and 'sleep tight,' how they kept insects out of their 'pie safes,' and where the preacher slept when he came to visit. The Tullie Smith House, lock, stock and barrel, provides the visitor with an invaluable portrait of rural life in Dekalb County (the farm's original site) before the Civil War.

The **Swan House**, toured next, presents another of Atlanta's many incarnations. Built in 1928 for cotton broker Edward Hamilton Inman and designed by Philip Trammell Shutze, the Swan could not be further from the Tullie Smith in ambience and values. Set in a 25-acre 'Italian' park, the architecture features a dramatic cascade (which echoes that of Rome's Villa Corsini) and horseshoe staircase, a Doric portico and arrival court straight out of 18th-century England, and swan motifs repeated throughout, not to mention the opulent Philip Trammell Shutze Collection of Decorative Arts. If you are famished and can't wait for lunch at Under-

ground Atlanta, there is the **Swan Coach House Restaurant** (Monday to Saturday 11.30am–2.30pm), which is a favorite with Atlanta ladies, tel: 404-261-0636.

This first day's itinerary is designed for the energetic. If you are getting a late start or would prefer a more leisurely day you may want to postpone the afternoon junket till another day.

If you are game, however, take your hotel shuttle bus (or park your rental car in the East Paces Ferry Road free MARTA parking lot and walk) to the Lenox NE7 MARTA station. Board a south-bound train and get off at the Five Points station downtown. Take two escalators up to street level, following signings for **Underground Atlanta**. If you lose your way, ask at MARTA's information booth to be directed to the glass doors opening into the MARTA-Underground Atlanta tunnel, which takes you into the unique entertainment-and-shopping mall. There are informed Metro Atlanta police patrolling MARTA stations at all hours, and uniformed security officers throughout Underground Atlanta: do not hesitate to ask for directions or assistance. The history of the tri-level mall, today called Underground, is the history

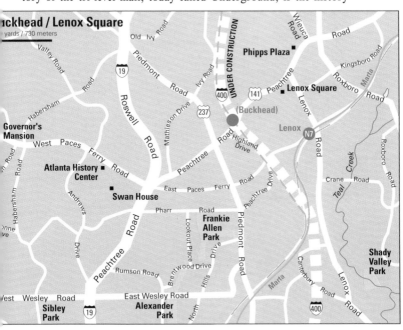

23

Underground's Orbitron

of a railroad-supplied mid-19th-century city literally buried alive by a skein of viaducts erected to span the railway's nexus and provide safe passage for early 20th-century pedestrian and automobile traffic attempting to cross 'Railroad Gulch.' Atlanta's post-bellum heart is now an entertainment complex comprising restaurants, nightclubs, chic boutiques, street vendors, 'theme statues' and fountains and, in season, a topsy-turvy ride called the Orbitron. The 19th-century city-beneath-the-city is a three-ring circus of fun that will draw you back on this and other afternoons to savor it to its fullest. For now, pick up a copy of *The Tracks of Underground Atlanta*, by Publication Concepts, and traverse the length of Lower Old Alabama Street – the entire length of Underground – exiting from the Kenny's Alley entranceway.

Underground Atlanta stores are open Monday to Friday 10am–9pm, Saturday and Sunday 11am–10pm; restaurants and bars have varying hours but during the weekend closing times are usually between midnight and 4am (Underground Atlanta Information: tel: 404-523-2311).

Diagonally across the square here, you will see **The World of Coca-Cola** pavilion, with its 12½-ton hanging neon bauble of a sign: unmistakable.

The World of Coca-Cola must be experienced to be believed, but it is a multi-layered cultural, or multi-cultural, experience as dense as, say, Disney World, the Pentagon or Stonehenge. It is also a

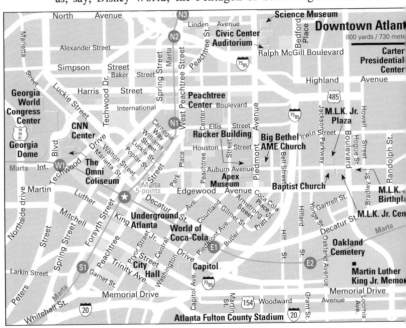

The World of Coca-Cola

multi-media advertising blitz featuring America's product-of-products, a museum documenting the history of American popular culture, an amusement park, a mini-college for students of creative advertising and marketing, a shrine, and a soda fountain. It can be taken as seriously as *Citizen Kane* or consumed as lightly as Diet Coke, but it is an Atlanta experience that must not be missed, and the darndest thing this travel writer has ever been through.

Of special note are the over 1,000 items of Coke memorabilia, a kinetic sculpture called the Bottling Fantasy, the futuristic soda fountain ('free' drinks for one and all), the 90-seat, high-definition television theater with its Coke-around-the-world video tour, and the Coca-Cola TradeMart for items of clothing and souvenirs featuring the world's best-known logo. It's on 55 Martin Luther King Jr Drive at Central Avenue, tel: 404-676-6074. Monday to Saturday 10am–9.30pm, Sunday noon–6pm; last entry one hour before closing; closed Easter, Thanksgiving, December 24, Christmas and New Year's Day; adults $2.50, seniors over 55 $2, children 6–12 $1.50, children under 6 free with adult admission; reservations advised at weekends and holidays.

After this beverage blitzkrieg, it's back to Underground Atlanta for shopping, snacking or simply strolling. Those who have not had their fill of history should seek out **Heritage Row** (55 Upper Alabama Street, tel: 404-584-7879. Tuesday to Saturday 10am–5pm, Sunday 1–5pm; closed Monday), where for a reasonable entrance fee, you can wander through six interactive exhibition halls chronicling important events in Atlanta's history, view a high-definition television presentation, and even climb into a Delta Air Lines Convair 880 cockpit.

If you are bound for the Underground Atlanta Danté's Down the Hatch for dinner and jazz featuring The Brothers Three

Exterior of Anthony's

preceded by a jazz pianist, you are in place for the evening – at least until about 1am, when the MARTA trains stop running. Those of you who have made reservations at Anthony's, the Buckhead Diner or Kamagawa should allow time to return to your hotels in Buckhead via MARTA.

Your destination this evening is **Anthony's** (3109 Piedmont Road NE, tel: 404-262-7379. Monday to Saturday 6–10.30pm), famed for its 'enlightened Southern cuisine.' Proceed by rental car south on Peachtree Road NE, and cross Piedmont Road NE. Turn left at the next traffic light into Maple Drive, then left at the next traffic light into East Paces Ferry Road; then right at the next traffic light into Piedmont Road NE again (avoiding a U-turn): Anthony's is half a block west on the right. There is valet parking.

The Georgian manse that houses the restaurant was originally built by English settlers in 1797, and was painstakingly moved, in 1964, brick by peg by plank, from Washington, Georgia to its present location. It is an absolutely authentic antebellum edifice: the former root cellar now serves as one of the two wine cellars and the original well-house structure and cooking ovens are also located on the property. Ask any of the staff to give you an impromptu guided tour and do not miss the bricks marked with bear paw prints. All of the original living areas have been transformed into intimately scaled dining areas. Anthony's has for many years running been named among America's 25 top dining establishments.

The most popular choice on the menu is titled 'Roasts Carved From Our Silver Chariot,' but seafood, fresh game and vegetarian selections may appeal to you. Hot soufflés like Orange Supreme, Chocolate Lovers or the Chef's Daily Special, are a tradition. The wine list has some 200 selections.

Dinner at eight

DAY 2

Cable News Network to Virginia-Highland

CNN Center, CNN Studio Tour, Georgia Dome; Jocks and Jills or Lenox Square for lunch; Virginia-Highland galleries; dinner at Indigo, The Dessert Place, or Dark Horse Tavern.

Begin this day with breakfast at your hotel, or get an earlier start and breakfast at the Omni. Have your hotel shuttle drop you off at MARTA's Lenox NE7 station. Take a south-bound train to the Five Points station and switch trains, taking a west-bound train one stop to the Omni-Dome-GA World Congress Center W1 station. Follow signings for CNN Center/Plaza Exit. At the top of the long escalator, turn right and enter CNN Center: follow signings for CNN Tour and purchase tickets at the CNN **Studio Tour** desk (tel: 404-827-2300; tickets go on sale at 8.30am daily; tours 9am–5pm, on the half hour, first come, first served; adults $6, seniors 65 and older $4, children 12 and under $3.50, children under 5 free).

CNN newsroom

Now is the time to head up another level in the Omni Hotel at CNN Center, where you can have breakfast at **The American Café at the Omni** (100 CNN Center; Level 2, tel: 404-818-4326. Breakfast Buffet 7–11am; à la carte breakfast till 11.30am), and look out into the glass and steel atrium of CNN Center, which houses Turner Broadcasting's Cable News Network studios, other diverse business offices, the Omni Hotel, restaurants and fast food snackeries, theatres, bars, and **The Turner Store**. (After your studio tour, you may or may not want to add another batch of logo-dusted T-shirts and other paraphernalia to your collection.) The tour itself will be especially fascinating for devotees of *Headline News* or CNN, as it takes you into the heart of the broadcasting studio where anchorpeople, writers, editors and producers are frenetically at work – little of this is ever seen on camera. What other newsroom in the world is

The Turner Store

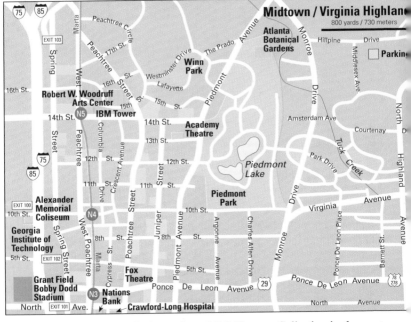

so honestly on display to its public? The TBS Collection is also part of the tour, featuring exhibits on CNN World Championship Wrestling, the MGM film acquisitions, etc. Make a note downstairs again of a 'sports bar' called **Jocks and Jills** (CNN Center, tel: 404-688-4225), the sports bar being a truly American phenomenon where you combine drinks or light meals with satellite-dish-beamed-in sporting events viewed on multiple screens.

You may want a bite here before or after your visit to the **Georgia Dome**. For the Dome, exit the CNN Center building and, keeping the Omni Arena on your left, proceed down International Boulevard (between the Omni and the Georgia World Congress Center) about a block and a half. The arena is where the Atlanta Hawks basketball team and the Atlanta Knights ice hockey team play in season, tel: 404-681-2100. The huge 'geodesic' dome (cream, plum and turquoise, a very '90s color scheme) straight ahead is your next destination (Georgia Dome, One Georgia Dome Drive NW, tel: 404-223-8600. Tours, on the hour, Tuesday to Saturday 10am–4pm, Sunday noon–4pm). It is a staggering experience: for me, it is the contemporary equivalent of seeing the Roman Coliseum, complete with lions and gladiators, from the point of view of a 1st-century Roman taxpayer (or Christian). The building cost 210 million dollars, is the largest cable-dome-stadium in the world, has enough air conditioning clout to cool 1,666 homes,

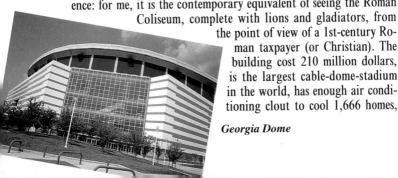

Georgia Dome

and generates enough wattage to light 13,000 more; seats more spectators than any stadium in the world except the Pontiac Silver Dome in Michigan, and could support a fully-loaded, four-wheel-drive pick-up truck on its teflon-coated fiberglass roof. The Dome hosts the Falcons' games in season, and such touring minstrels as U2 and Paul McCartney, motorcycle races, little affairs such as the 1994 Peach Bowl game, and is slated to showcase the 1996 Olympics gymnastic and basketball events. The suites staked out by season ticket moguls for about $120,000 per season are generally the jaw-dropper of the tour.

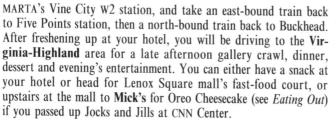

Ask your guide to direct you the block and a half to MARTA's Vine City W2 station, and take an east-bound train back to Five Points station, then a north-bound train back to Buckhead. After freshening up at your hotel, you will be driving to the **Virginia-Highland** area for a late afternoon gallery crawl, dinner, dessert and evening's entertainment. You can either have a snack at your hotel or head for Lenox Square mall's fast-food court, or upstairs at the mall to **Mick's** for Oreo Cheesecake (see *Eating Out*) if you passed up Jocks and Jills at CNN Center.

Beginning at the intersection of Lenox Road and Peachtree Road NE, take Lenox Road in an easterly direction towards Interstate 85 (I-85). It is just under 2 miles to the junction; take I-85 South (which involves a short detour down the Buford Highway, well-signed). Proceed south on I-85 to the Monroe Drive exit, a little less than a mile further on. Pass under the interstate, and take an immediate right into Monroe Drive NE. Cross Montgomery Ferry Drive NE and Piedmont Avenue; 2½ miles from I-85, take a sharp left into Virginia Avenue. About a mile further on, turn left into North Highland Avenue NE. (This intersection forms the hub of the Greenwich-Village-like Virginia-Highland area, and you will be returning here after dinner, so take note.) Approximately 4200ft up Highland Avenue is the **Highland Walk shopping center**, on your left, and two good, small art galleries you may want to investigate prior to dinner across the street at either Indigo or Partners. The **Modern Primitive Gallery** (1402 North Highland Avenue, tel: 404-892-0556. Tuesday to Thursday 11.30am–9pm, Friday and Saturday 11.30am–10pm, Sunday 1–9pm) is a cornucopia of color, with

Patio of Indigo Grill

works divided into the categories of folk art, primitive, outsider, self-directed and visionary, providing a glimpse of a very different side of Atlanta, Georgia and America.

Aliya, in the same shopping center (tel: 404-892-2835; Monday to Thursday 2–10pm, Friday 2–11pm, Saturday 11.30am–11pm, Sunday noon–10pm) presents more mainstream if not more decorative works, by both local and international artists: ceramics and drawings predominate, and the work of as many as 45 artists is on show simultaneously. Across the street is **Indigo Coastal Grill** ('Where Bland is Banned') or, if Indigo is jam-packed, **Partners Café**, located next door (1397 and 1399 North Highland Avenue, tels: 404-875-0202/404-876-0676 respectively: neither restaurant accepts reservations, so record your name at the door and wait to be called).

Naughty but nice

Indigo's décor is slate-board-menu/Caribbean, and the seafood is superb: baked-in-parchment fish filets, the Beach Steamer of lobster, mussels and clams, Calamari Wok, etc. Partners has more than a touch of Paris-minimalist-chic married to Aix-en-Hockney-smart, is a whole other culinary scene, but just as surprising and good. Pasta specials, fowl-by-way-of-South-East Asia and Manhattan: both restaurants' menus are mercurial and creative. These eateries have much in common with the galleries across the street. Just show up at any of these places with plastic money, and enjoy yourself.

After dinner, forego dessert if you can – or plan to have two – and retrace your tracks just under a mile back down North Highland Avenue to **The Dessert Place** (1000 Virginia Avenue, tel: 404-892-8921. Monday to Thursday 11am–11.30pm, Friday and Saturday 11am–12.30am, Sunday 1–11.30pm). Order the Hot Fudge Cream Cheese Brownie or the Chocolate Caramel Pie à la Mode, with coffee, and sit on the verandah. You will have time after dessert to shop or window-shop here in Virginia-Highland, an area hip-deep in boutiques, antique shops, cafés and clubs.

Go by **Corner Compact Disc** (1048 North Highland Avenue NE, tel: 404-875-3087) and ask to hear recordings by some of Georgia's finest recording artists. A partial list: TLC, Kriss Kross, REM, B-52s, Indigo Girls, Kristen Hall, Wendy Bucklew, Cicada Sings, Insane Jane, Caroline Aiken, Hip Heavy Lip, Michelle Malone and Murray Attaway. Keep this list in mind when you peruse Saturday's *Atlanta Journal-Constitution* and *Creative Loafing* for who's playing live where in the city. I caught Kristin Hall at Eddie's Attic, accompanied by an Indigo Girl no less, the last time I was in town. After all is said and done, seen and eaten, there's the **Dark Horse Tavern** (816 North Highland Avenue, tel: 404-873-3607), with bands, locals and darts downstairs. Then, time to go home.

Nightowls with more literary interests should remember that both **Oxford Book Stores** (2345 Peachtree Street NE and 360 Pharr Road, tels: 404-364-2700/262-3333) are open Sunday to Thursday till midnight; Friday and Saturday till 2am. These are marvelous book emporia, complete with **Cup and Chaucer** cafés, local, national and international magazines and a diverse, literate clientele with whom to strike up conversation. The stores are great places to meet Atlantans.

DAY 3

African-American Atlanta

Saturday Atlanta Preservation Center tour of 'Sweet' Auburn Avenue; African-American Panoramic Experience (APEX) Museum; the Martin Luther King Jr Center For Nonviolent Social Change, Inc; Martin Luther King Jr Birth Home; Auburn Avenue Rib Shack. If you're in town on a Sunday, don't miss a service at Ebenezer Baptist Church.

You will want to phone the **Atlanta Preservation Center** for information regarding their **Sweet Auburn/MLK District Tour**, a very reasonably priced, guided walking tour of Auburn Avenue in downtown Atlanta, the heart of the city's first prosperous African-American community. It's also the site of the King Center, the tomb of Martin Luther King Jr, the former Civil Rights leader's childhood home, and the church where both he and his father were pastors. The Atlanta Preservation Center (The DeSoto, Suite 3, 156 7th Street NE, tel: 404-876-2040) is a city-wide, non-profit making membership organization which is dedicated to promoting historic preservation in Atlanta through education and advocacy, and this and their other tours are a walker's delight.

The 'Sweet Auburn' tour is usually scheduled

Dr Martin Luther King, Jr

for Saturday mid-morning, and the rendezvous is the APEX Museum. If the tour is set for 11am, you may want to schedule an hour to reach the APEX from Buckhead, which will leave you time to investigate the APEX Museum's modest collection of African-American art and memorabilia, and to view the short documentary on Auburn Avenue and the Civil Rights movement which shows in the APEX auditorium. The tour itself lasts about an hour and a half; longer if you tour both the King Center and the MLK Birth Home.

In summer, please come prepared with a hat, some sun-block and a pair of walking shoes to make your walk more comfortable. As on the Virginia-Highland segment of your Day 2 Itinerary, you should proceed by rental car from the Lenox/Peachtree roads intersection down Lenox Road to I-85, and head south (towards the skyscrapers of downtown Atlanta). I-85 merges with I-75: 5½ miles from the Lenox Road exit, turn off at the Courtland Street exit, No 97 and after about 3600ft turn left into Auburn Avenue.

Apex Museum

The **APEX Museum** (135 Auburn Avenue NE, tel: 404-521-APEX. June-August: Tuesday to Saturday 10am–5pm, Wednesday 10am–6pm, Sunday 1–5pm, closed Monday; adults $2, students and seniors $1) is a small storefront building on your right: there should be plenty of parking in front, or just behind the building.

Dwarfed by the Fulton County African-American Research Library at the corner of Auburn Avenue and Courtland Street, the APEX is only phase one of an ambitious museum project, the new building being scheduled to open prior to the Olympics. Phase two should document the African-American experience from the first slave to the Space Age. Before setting out with your group, do tell the guide you are interested in touring the Martin Luther King Jr Birth Home: you will need to

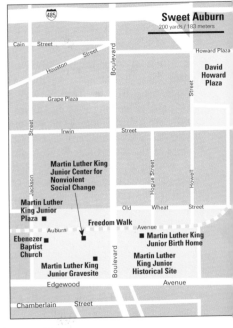

Family outing

phone in advance from APEX (tel: 404-331-3920) in order to reserve a place on that tour.

Your walking tour now sets off down Auburn Avenue, once a Cherokee trail leading from a burial ground in Lawrenceville to a pow wow site in what is now Atlanta's Five Points area. The early 19th-century German-American community which gave the avenue its first name – Wheat Street – was supplanted by an African-American residential community, after early 20th-century race riots and the advent of the Jim Crow laws, which segregated the city into 'white or colored' wards. The wealth and social status engendered by prominent African-American financial institutions which sprang up on the avenue may have been responsible for adding the 'sweetness' to 'Sweet Auburn.'

There is no doubt that Auburn Avenue was a real showcase for African-American Atlantans' will to succeed, despite all odds, from the 1930s onward. Highlights of the tour are the offices of the *Atlanta Daily World*, the newspaper which, opening in 1932, became the first African-American daily to be published in the United States. The **Royal Peacock Club**, originally the Top Hat Club, which opened in 1930, and whose 'Egyptian Revival' interior resembles that of the Egyptian Ballroom at the Fox Theatre, has experienced several renaissances: during the 1960s, such African-American greats as James Brown, Otis Redding, the Supremes and B B King all performed here, to the delight of packed, racially-mixed audiences.

Auburn is also home to the **Big Bethel AME Church**, Atlanta's first African-American church, founded in the mid-1800s; the Gothic-revival Wheat Street Baptist Church,

Big Bethel AME Church

founded in 1870; and, of course, **Ebenezer Baptist Church**, which opened on Auburn in 1922, and where 'Daddy' King, and his illustrious son Martin Luther King Jr, served as pastors. The **King Center's Freedom Hall Complex**, founded by Coretta Scott King and Christine King Farris in 1982, houses the most extensive collection of Martin Luther King Jr memorabilia in the world, and is the site of King's tomb and Eternal Flame.

Set in a 'Meditation Pool' meant to evoke eastern Indian architecture – a reminder of Ghandi's influence on the Civil Rights leader – the simple, white Georgia marble crypt is inscribed: Rev. Martin Luther King, Jr; 1929–1968; 'Free at last. Free at last. Thank God Almighty I'm Free at last.'

The last stop on your Auburn Avenue tour proper is the King Center. Just up the street, if you are taking the tour of the **Martin Luther King Jr Birth Home** is the Queen Anne-style house where King was born and spent his boyhood. Built in the 1890s, and purchased by King's maternal grandfather, the Rev. Alfred Daniel Williams, in 1909, the house has been restored and furnished so as to provide a touchingly human portrait of the life and times on affluent but pious Sweet Auburn when King was a young, often irreverent boy (501 Auburn Avenue; June to Labor Day daily, 10am–4.30pm; Labor Day to May 9am–7.30pm; free admission).

From 'Daddy' King's hat and coat on the hatrack to the crib

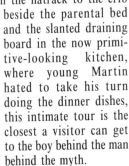

beside the parental bed and the slanted draining board in the now primitive-looking kitchen, where young Martin hated to take his turn doing the dinner dishes, this intimate tour is the closest a visitor can get to the boy behind the man behind the myth.

After this mini-tour provided by the National Park Service, you may want to head back to the **King Center** (449 Auburn Avenue, tel: 404-524-1956. Monday to Friday 9am–5.30pm; weekends 10am–5.30pm) for a more leisurely look at some of the exhibits, the crypt or the bookstore, which is a fine source of Martin Luther King Jr's writings as well as other books on

Martin Luther King, Jr home

Auburn Rib Shack

the Civil Rights movement and non-violent social change in general.

If you want to investigate other sites of specifically African-American Atlanta, you should pick up a small book titled *Scenes of Black Atlanta: A Full Color Pictorial Guide and Location Directory* at the bookstore. Between mid-June and the end of August, the King Center is the focal point of the **Kingfest**, an annual program of scheduled performances by local, national and international classical, blues, soul, jazz and gospel artists which is certainly worth checking out (Kingfest Hotline, tel: 404-662-4560).

Tired and hungry? Stop in at a national politicians' favorite haunt: the **Auburn Rib Shack** (302 Auburn Avenue, tel: 404-523-8315. Tuesday to Wednesday 11.30am–5pm, Thursday 11.30am–6pm, Friday and Saturday 11.30am–10pm; closed Sunday and Monday) and order either beef or pork barbecued ribs, the house specialty; or such daily specials as ox-tail, short ribs or smothered chicken wings; plus desserts like peach cobbler, apple pie and sweet potato pie. (Vegetarians may want to head up the street to **The Beautiful Restaurant**, located at 397 Auburn Avenue.)

Since this itinerary can be physically and emotionally demanding, this is a good evening to spend swimming till dusk in your hotel's pool, then dining out, light, at a place like **The Peasant Uptown**.

Auburn Avenue attitude

You may want to squeeze in a new film at one of Phipps Plaza's or Lenox Square's multiple cinemas as well, or sample humor served up hot at **The Punch Line** in Sandy Springs (see *Eating Out* and *Nightlife* sections for more details).

If you have time during your stay, you may want to pay a visit to the 1910 mansion which was home to the late Alonzo F Herndon, founder of the Atlanta Life Insurance Company and an illustrious African-American Atlantan (587 University Place NW, tel: 404-581-9813. Tuesday to Saturday tours on the hour 10am–4pm). Gray Line of Atlanta also offers a comprehensive 3½-hour tour titled **Black Heritage Tour** (tel: 404-767-0594, Saturday only).

Ebenezer Baptist Church

Sunday Service at Ebenezer Baptist Church

If you do nothing else in Atlanta, show up at this simple, unpretentious church, pastored for 80 years by members of the King family, and attend the 7.45am service on Sunday morning.

If you have never attended a Baptist church service, or if you are familiar with less charismatic, less emotionally charged services than those at Ebenezer, the 'sound and fury' of the music, the high-decibel delivery of the liturgy and the responsiveness of the congregation may, initially, come as something of a shock to your more coolly Protestant, more regimented Catholic, more contemplatively Buddhist sensibilities.

But if you come, dressed in your Sunday best (suits, hats if you have them, ties, heels), and open your hearts and minds to this remarkable group of true believers, I think you will come away with a deep understanding of the African-American heritage shared by all Americans, of the deeply spiritual heritage shared by all African-Americans and of the particular heritage of faith, service and selflessness which is shared by the King family in particular, and their church in general. Simply listening and, yes, gently rocking and rolling, to the Martin Luther King Choir for an hour and a half is a revelation.

Follow directions on page 32, and proceed to 407/413 Auburn Avenue. If you arrive a little early, you will usually be allowed to proceed directly to the sanctuary, which is always pleasantly air-conditioned. Groups will want to call ahead (tel: 404-688-7263) to reserve several pews. The church is also open to the public Monday to Friday 9am–5.30pm. Founded in 1886 by the Rev. John Andrew Parker, the present structure was built between 1914–22 under the Rev. Alfred Daniel Williams, the maternal grandfather of Martin Luther King Jr. In 1931, Dr King Sr, son-in-law of Williams, took over as pastor. Martin Luther King Jr was a co-pastor with his father at Ebenezer church from 1960 till his death in 1968.

Work is a pleasure

Keep working for
the LORD.

PICK & MIX

Morning tour of the Fox Theatre in midtown, lunch at the Chefs' Grill, then the High Museum of Art.

You will be using MARTA for this day-time excursion. Board a south-bound train at the Lenox NE7 station, exiting at the North Avenue N3 station. Ascend the stairs and turn left: exit into Ponce de Leon Avenue and turn right. The **Fox Theatre** (660 Peachtree Street, tel: 404-876-2041, Box Office 404-249-6400. Tours Monday and Thursday 10am, Saturday 10 and 11.30am) is located at the corner of Ponce de Leon Avenue and Peachtree Street NE.

'The Fabulous Fox,' saved in the mid-1970s by a vociferous fund-raising campaign, started life in 1929 as a (Shriners') Yaarab Temple then, shortly, a movie palace. It still has a mixed civic-religious feel to it, what with its onion domes, minarets and little movie marquees: a sort of Arabian Nights meets Brighton Beach. It is a grand structure, and your guided tour highlights all the elegant tricks of acoustics, sunrise and sunset lighting effects, complete with starry sky, etc.

When your Fox tour ends, board a north-bound MARTA train for the Arts Center N5 station. Take three escalators up, following signings for the **Woodruff Arts Center**. A flight of stairs and covered archways will take you directly to the center, home of the Atlanta Symphony Orchestra and the Alliance Theater, among other worthies. But first, lunch.

Inside the Woodruff Arts Center is the **Chefs' Grill** (1280 Peachtree Street NE, tel: 404-881-0652. Monday to Friday lunch 11.30am–2.30pm, Tuesday to Saturday dinner 5.30pm–closing time varying with the center performances; reservations urged). The menu here is 'fresh seasonal American,' and chef Michael Gravely recommends crab cakes with tomato ginger sauce, the smoked chicken, shrimp and corn salad and the daily pizza special, with wine by the glass. For dessert, try fresh blackberry pound cake. This is also the place to

Artistic expression

High Museum of Art

reserve a table before or after Atlanta Symphony, Alliance Theater or Atlanta Opera Company performances. Come to the Chefs' Grill for drinks alone, for starters, full meals, or a post-performance dessert.

The **High Museum of Art** (1280 Peachtree Street NE, tel: 404-892-3600. Tuesday to Thursday 10am–5pm, Friday 10am–9pm, Saturday 10am–5pm, Sunday noon–5pm; closed Monday; adults $5, students and seniors over 65 $3, children 6–17 $1, under six free, free Thursday 1–5pm) is the next stop. Architect Richard Meier's radiant, reflective 'crystal' clad in porcelain-enameled steel panels was irreverently nicknamed 'the shower stall' when it first went up in the early 1980s. But it has since commanded the respect it merits, and the copy-cat Swissotel in Buckhead proves imitation is the sincerest form of flattery.

The High provides 46,000sq ft of gallery space, and the permanent collection is eclectic, diverse rich gifts having created significant holdings of sub-Saharan African, European, American, 20th-century and decorative art. Of special interest is the Uhry Print Collection, with works by French Impressionists and Post Impressionists, German Expressionists and American 20th-century artists.

The excellent **gift shop** – in its own right a shoppers' destination in Atlanta – sells a catalogue of selected works, which will familiarize newcomers with the museum's range: tours are on offer as well. My own favorite works are modern/contemporary, including the High's superb collection of photography, much of it on show along with folk art at the museum's **Downtown Galleries** (Georgia-Pacific Center, 133 Peachtree Street, tel: 404-577-6940. Monday to Friday 11am–5pm, closed Memorial Day, May 31; free admission). Enquire at the front desk about temporary exhibits, and pick up a plan of the museum which maps out the collections. Remember: the gift shop closes 15 minutes before the galleries.

The High's 'Garden in Sochi' by Arshville Gorky

Goldberg bagel breakfast; the Chattahoochee Nature Center; Historic Roswell; Bulloch Hall Tour; lunch at The Public House; shopping at the Roswell Mill.

From the Lenox Road/Peachtree Road NE intersection, proceed in a south-westerly direction down Peachtree, passing the Ritz-Carlton on your right. Stay on Peachtree, crossing through the Piedmont Road NE intersection. After about a mile, turn right into tiny Sardis Way NE, which immediately becomes Roswell Road. After about 2½ miles, turn right again into the **Roswell Wieuca Shopping Center** and stop at the **Goldberg & Son, Inc. Bagel Bakery-Delicatessen** (tel: 404-256-3751; Monday 7am–3pm, Tuesday to Thursday 7am–5pm, Friday 7am–6pm, Saturday 7am–5pm, Sunday 7am–4pm).

Goldberg's has received *Atlanta Magazine* awards for the best bagels in the city: there are ten varieties, and the cinnamon-raisin's great for breakfast. (The Goldbergs' motto? It's on the menu: 'Judgement and good taste pass through our doors every day – our customers!') Exit back into Roswell and turn right, heading north-east.

Goldberg's Deli

Proceed for about 2½ miles, and pass over I-285. Continue on Roswell. After 10 miles, you will cross the Chattahoochee River via the Archie L Lindsay Memorial Bridge. Take an immediate left into Azalea Drive. The river will be on your left and you will pass the Chattahoochee River Park, where it is possible to rent canoes. After about 1½ miles, turn left into Willeo Road and proceed for half a mile. Turn right into the parking lot of the **Chattahoochee Nature Center** (913 Willeo Road, Roswell, tel: 404-992-2055. Monday to Saturday 9am–5pm, Sunday noon–5pm; minimal admission fee).

This non-profit, environmental education facility is located on a 130-acre site in the Chattahoochee River Corridor, where indigenous flora and fauna abound, as well as endangered species rescued from all over Georgia. Director Greg Greer advises first-time visitors to take a leisurely exploratory stroll along the **woodland** or **wetland trails**, experiencing nature first-hand. Saturday and Sunday at 1 and 3pm there are walks guided by naturalists. Every Tuesday evening, April through October, there is a Chattahoochee River Canoe Float scheduled, 24 participants at a time: Mr Greer favors October, when the mist makes the river a photographer's dream: book in advance. There is also a road race called The Possum Trot sponsored by the center, for runners visiting in June, but

Chattahoochee Nature Center

call ahead for a complete schedule of center activities if this
sort of thing interests you.

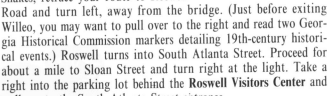

While you are here, observe the
pond with binoculars and identify, with a little help, perhaps,
some 25 bird species. The gift shop
on the premises is a child's delight:
toys, authentic replicas of ocean
mammals and dinosaurs – as well as
bird feeders, books on nature, jewelry, etc. After an hour or so with
Eastern Screech Owls and Yellow Rat
Snakes, retrace your route to Roswell
Road and turn left, away from the bridge. (Just before exiting
Willeo, you may want to pull over to the right and read two Georgia Historical Commission markers detailing 19th-century historical events.) Roswell turns into South Atlanta Street. Proceed for
about a mile to Sloan Street and turn right at the light. Take a
right into the parking lot behind the **Roswell Visitors Center** and
walk up to the South Atlanta Street entrance.

Roswell, founded in 1839, was largely spared from destruction
during the Civil War, and there are numerous examples of extant
antebellum architecture here in the historic city center which merit
either a house tour or a walking tour. Get details on times at the
center, where an informative video introducing you to the city will
familiarize you with touring, dining, shopping and bed and breakfast options. **Major James Bulloch's stately home** would be my
own choice today. This Greek Revival mansion, complete with slave
quarters and barn, was the childhood home of Mittie Bulloch, wife
of Theodore Roosevelt. Following your tour, stop in for lunch at
The Public House (605 South Atlanta Street, tel: 404-992-4646.
Monday to Friday 11.30am–2.30pm, Saturday and Sunday
11.30am–3pm, Sunday to Thursday 5.30–10pm, Friday and Saturday 5.30–11pm). A member of the Peasant chain, The Public
House's service and standards are above reproach.

After lunch mosey, Southern style, down South Atlanta Street,
stopping in shops on your way. The **Roswell Mill**
(85 Mill Street, tel: 404-642-6140) – take
your car if it is a blazing day – is
about five minutes downhill.

The original mill structure
that stood here was built in
1838, but razed by Sherman in
1864 and rebuilt in 1882.
Today, a sort of historic shopping mall houses gift shops,
restaurants, cafés and craftspeople displaying their wares.

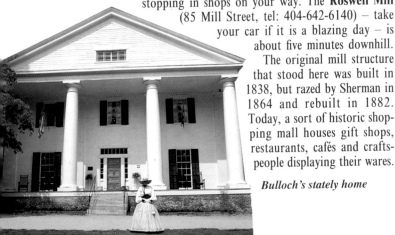

Bulloch's stately home

3. The Fernbank Museum

A visit to a museum of the future.

To reach today's destination, take Lenox Road/Cheshire Bridge Road NE towards I-85, but pass under the interstate highway and forge ahead. At the second traffic light turn left into LaVista Road NE. After about half a mile turn right at the first light, into Shepherds Lane then, after a similar distance, right into Briarcliff Road; take an immediate left at the first light, into Clifton Road. Pass the Centers for Disease Control and Prevention on your right, and then Emory University. Stay on Clifton and about 3 miles further on turn left into the Fernbank Museum

The **Fernbank Museum of Natural History** and the Fernbank Science Center's Jim Cherry Memorial **Planetarium**, along with the **Fernbank Forest**, comprise something much more than a museum because the word doesn't begin to express or describe the experiential arc of Fernbank. It's a museum of the future, and one of the most exciting and attractive laboratories of the mind and senses in the United States, if not the world – especially educational and exciting if you are traveling with school-age children. The physical structure of the building itself is worth an architectural tour.

Designed by Graham Gund Associates of Cambridge, Massachusetts, the Fernbank is floored in fossil-rich limestone quarried in the Solnhofen Quarry, near Nürnberg, Germany. The permanent exhibits include **Spectrum of the Senses**, 65 hands-on, inter-active exhibits which focus on the physical laws of sight and sound – the gallery whirring and flashing and spinning with lights, computer-images, lasers, and the intense voices of children at work and play, at their various levels of ability.

A Walk Through Time in Georgia, whose 15 galleries (each a gem created by naturalists, taxidermists and multi-media artists) propel visitors through the ecosystems of Georgia and, simultaneously, the chronological development of the planet, is a sort of university in miniature. The **IMAX Theater**, its six-story screen displaying films such as *Mountain Gorilla* and *Grand Canyon* (and, believe me, you are *there*) is another highlight of the museum's holdings. And, yes, there are permanent collections, such as the **World of Shells**, but it is the mercurial quest for knowledge that gets embodied, and communicated in this 'exploratorium,' more than anything you can catalogue.

Fernbank Museum

Do not miss the **Fernbank Museum Store**, with its science books, nature learning kits, plush mammoth and triceratops toys, cassettes of whale and porpoise song and flora-and-fauna-jewelry. And, if you decide to spend the whole day here, there's an attractive cafeteria on the lower level.

Dinosaur Hall

The museum (767 Clifton Rd NE, tel: 404-378-0127) is open Monday to Saturday 9am–6pm, Sunday noon–6pm, closed Thanksgiving and Christmas; adults $5.50, students/seniors $4.50; open evenings for special films, programs. The planetarium (156 Heaton Park Drive NE, tel: 404-378-4311) is open Monday 8.30am–5pm; Tuesday to Friday 8.30am–10pm, Sunday 1–5pm; also some evenings when the weather is clear; adults $2, students $1.

Those of you who want to forage a little further afield should now head left out into Clifton Road again. After a mile, turn right into Ponce de Leon Avenue and after another mile turn left into Moreland Avenue NE. Half a mile further on on your right is a small, unpretentious-looking café and night-spot called **Eat Your Vegetables**. The hours are complex (tel: 404-523-2671; Monday to Saturday lunch 11.30am–3pm, Sunday brunch 11am–3pm, Sunday to Thursday dinner 6–10pm, Friday and Saturday dinner 6–10.30pm, daily light fare and coffee bar 3–6pm, Thursday to Sunday live entertainment 10pm–2am) but the food's a vegetarian's dream: everything from Veggie Burgers through Spinach Wellington, and five specialties daily.

Carnivores inspired by Fernbank's Dinosaur Hall may want to head across the street to the **Star Community Bar** to order from its 'Elvis Menu' or 'Elvez Menu' (Tex-Mex): either way, you will want to return to both these attractive, laid-back venues in the evening for the music (see *Nightlife* section).

Star Community Bar

A day away from the city to visit the largest bas-relief carving in the world, plus an antebellum plantation. Bring your swimsuit. Alternatively, ride the dinner train to Stone Mountain.

To get to Stone Mountain from Atlanta, take I-85 north to 'the Perimeter' and proceed south on I-285 towards Macon/Augusta. Proceed for just over 5 miles and exit, following signs for Stone Mountain Park, at Exit 30b, Highway 78 East/410. Five miles further on you will see the massif of Stone Mountain ahead of you: almost 8 miles from I-285 on 78E/410, exit to Stone Mountain Park's East Gate Entrance (right lane exit, by the way). Cross Stone Mountain Lake, with the monolith on your left. Bear left towards Memorial Hall and turn left into Memorial Drive (Stone Mountain Park, Highway 78, Stone Mountain, tel: 404-498-5600. The park's attractions are open June to August 10am–9pm; September to May 10am–5.30pm; admission $5 per car, plus individual attraction tickets).

Given a natural wonder such as **Stone Mountain**, the world's largest exposed granite monolith, Ansel Adams would have set up a tripod for his camera (as he did for Yosemite's Half Dome in 1960). The Daughters of the Confederacy, not having a great deal in common with the Ansel Adamses of this world, envisioned something else altogether. When they and their chosen sculptors were through with the 7,532,750,950-cubic-foot block of virgin granite, it would bear, for all time, the high-relief likenesses of Confederate President Jefferson Davis and Generals Robert E

Stone Mountain carving

Lee and 'Stonewall' Jackson: a sort of painstakingly executed, indelible *graffito*, and the largest bas-relief carving in the world – much more permanent than the beautiful, simple soapstone bowls and dishes left near the site by the indigenous peoples who lived beneath this natural 'acropolis' some 5,000 years ago.

Whatever today's eco-visitor makes of such patriotic statements in stone as Mount Rushmore and Stone Mountain, they are indeed sights to see, and **Stone Mountain Park** is a special venue in that, apart from the gigantic sculpture on view, there is a cable-car ascent to the top of the 825ft-high monolith; a working railroad that traverses a five-mile course around the mountain, taking in en route pristine north Georgia flora and fauna; an antebellum plantation of the 1800s with 19 original buildings transplanted here from else-

Stone Mountain Lake

where in the state; a paddlewheel riverboat which cruises 363-acre **Stone Mountain Lake**; an Antique Auto and Music Museum; a nightly May-through-Labor Day (weekends through October) laser show; wildlife trails; two golf courses; white sand shores along the lake, perfect for mid-summer swimming and water sports; tennis, concerts, jogging etc, etc – plus the **Stone Mountain Inn** (tel: 404-469-3311, toll free 800-277-0007).

I would suggest calling ahead for general information about concerts or special events scheduled during your stay, and then driving out, prepared with bathing costume and towel, to spend the day, planning on a cable-car **Skylift** trip to the top of the mountain; a visit to the Antebellum Plantation; a river boat cruise; a few hours at the beach, and then round of the day with dinner at The Mountain View Restaurant and taking in the laser show from Memorial Lawn. The 'Big Ticket' (adults $12.50, children $8.50) admits you to six attractions, and beats adding up individual fares. Proceed to the Ticket and Information Center at **Memorial Hall**; view the museum while you are there and stop in at the gift shop next door for booklets on the park and Civil War collectibles and books (daily 9.30am–9.30pm).

Especially interesting to foreign visitors, above and beyond the park's considerable recreational facilities, is the **Antebellum Plantation**. It was the aim of the Stone Mountain Memorial Association, responsible for developing the park, to 'illustrate how a well-to-do family lived in the period between 1820 and 1860,' on the eve of what many Southerners still persist in calling 'The War Between The States,' or 'The War of Northern Aggression.' The buildings in this complex admirably fulfill this mission. From the 1830s **Country Store**, moved to Stone Mountain from Orange, Georgia, to the **Thornton House**, built in 1790, and perhaps the oldest restored house in Georgia, and the **Main House**, built in the

Laser show, Stone Mountain

1840s near Dickey, Georgia, and slave cabins, originally part of the Graves Plantation near Covington, Georgia, this reconstructed plantation accurately reflects a way of life that is 'gone with the wind.' The interiors have been meticulously furnished with priceless period antiques: rooms such as the **Kingston House**'s 'Borning Room,' the free-standing 'Necessary House' (or 'outhouse'), and the implement-filled barn complex buildings will bring alive America's 'era of plantations' in a way the written word cannot. Just outside the park's West Gate is **Stone Mountain Village**, a real hamlet which, though a bit cutesy and craftsy, is pretty much an authentically southern main street town of the last century. The Stone Mountain Village Welcome Center is located in a candy-apple-red caboose at 891 Main Street. Stone Mountain shops are open Monday to Saturday 10am–5pm; Sunday 1–5pm; tel: 404-296-8058 or 404-879-9511 for further information.

Dinner Train to Stone Mountain

At weekends from May through November (the very limited schedule varies), the **New Georgia Railroad** (The Georgia Building Authority, 1 Martin Luther King Jr Drive, tel: 404-656-0769. Monday to Friday 8.30am–4.30pm), a restored vintage train, makes a memorable dinner run from the Milepost Station near Underground Atlanta.

Board the train and take your seat in one of the grand old dining cars. Over the 2½-hour journey out to Stone Mountain Village and back, enjoy your tenderloin, chicken teriyaki or sole, plus starters, assorted desserts – wine or spirits you bring along yourself – while you watch historic Oakland Cemetery, the Martin Luther King Jr Center, Agnes Scott College and other Atlanta landmarks pass your window. You can reach **Milepost Station** by taking MARTA to the Five Points station and crossing Underground Atlanta (see *Day 1 Itinerary*), but in evening dress you may opt for a taxi instead.

The train departs at 7.30pm: boarding time is 7pm sharp. Bring chilled champagne: your attentive, white-jacketed waiter will provide an ice bucket. (Excursions to Savannah, Georgia and Chattanooga, Tennessee are also available.)

Dinner train

A perfect opportunity for athletic visitors to hike in pristine north Georgia woodlands, tour an historic Civil War battlefield and visit an excellent small archeological museum detailing early Native American settlements in the area. Dress for a hike: proper boots, hat, canteen of water, a picnic lunch packed by your hotel or Goldberg's Deli – and a field guide to indigenous flora and fauna, available at the park's Visitors' Center. (Note: there are poisonous plants and snakes in the region. Rangers will acquaint you with any dangers you might encounter.)

Ask your hotel concierge the fastest way, for the time and day, of reaching I-75 North (heading towards Chattanooga, Tennessee). This may involve taking West Paces Ferry Road or Lenox Road to I-85/Downtown. About 10 miles north of the Perimeter on I-75, exit at the Highway 41/Barrett Parkway/Kennesaw Exit 116; 1½ miles further on, turn right into Highway 41/Cobb Parkway, and follow signs for **Kennesaw Mountain National Battlefield Park**. Turn left at the light into Old 41 Highway NW, entering the park after about a mile. Turn in at the entrance to the Visitors' Center/Park Headquarters (tel: 404-427-4686; daily 8.30am –5pm, Saturday and Sunday 8.30am–6pm).

Kennesaw National Battlefield

A well-scripted slide presentation at the center is the best introduction to the park, recounting the events of the Battle of Kennesaw Mountain in June of 1864. It was the cruellest siege of the Atlanta Campaign, pitting an unknown number of the Union's 100,000 men and their 254 pieces of artillery under General William T Sherman, against the Confederacy's 50,000 soldiers and 187 cannon, under the command of General Joseph E Johnston. Three thousand Union and 800 Confederate casualties resulted, mainly at the battle site known as Cheatham Hill. Sherman, repulsed, resorted to outflanking maneuvers but pushed on south: two months later, on September 2, 1864, Atlanta fell.

The small but well-presented collection of Civil War artifacts is another feature of the center. Military uniforms worn by both armies, fife and drum, flags, maps, a physician's field kit, swords, shells, muskets, bayonets and cannon all bring the conflict alive. An excellent selection of Civil War books is for sale, in addition to field guides to the Georgia mountains. The 2,884-acre National Park, where the Confederates briefly halted Sherman's drive to Atlanta, preserves the battleground, earthwork trenches and the natural beauty of this area of north Georgia. The park's 16 miles of **hiking trails** – well mapped and marked, with facilities for picnicking – make the 2-, 5-, 10- and 16-mile hikes a pleasure for naturalists. A self-guiding automobile tour taking in **Kennesaw Mountain**, with its panoramic view of the surrounding terrain, as well as the battle sites of **Pigeon Hill**, **Cheatham Hill** and **Kolb's Farm** can take less than an hour to complete. You may wish to phone ahead to see whether your visit coincides with any of the events in the park's 'Interpretive Schedule,' which include rifle and artillery demonstrations, lectures and demonstrations on such topics as Civil War medicine, African-Americans in the Civil War, etc.

There are two routes north to **Cartersville**, some 20 miles up I-75 from Kennesaw. The easiest route is via the interstate highway. Follow signs for Cartersville Main Street/Etowah Indian Mounds and exit off I-75 at Exit 124. (The scenic route, via Highway 41, is less clearly marked, and this writer got herself lost in rural horse-breeding country in the heat of a summer's day. As is true throughout the rural south, off the interstates, signs are often non-existent, and locals are not accustomed to giving visitors accurate directions: play it safe and take main roads.) Well signposted from Main Street in Cartersville, the **Etowah Indian Mounds State Historic Site** is only a few miles outside town.

The Native Americans who inhabited this region from about AD1000 till the mid-1500s, culturally related by material goods, ideas, ceremonies and language, are known to archeologists as the **Mississippian Culture**. This north Georgia river valley site was home to the corn-growing Etowah people, and was rich in the cherts they used for tools, in sweet acorns, hickory nuts, walnuts, small game and, most crucial, sandy loam alluvial soil. The museum

Battle of Kennesaw Mountain

on the site details the
life of the Mississippian
Culture, including the
people's tools, distinc-
tive artifacts, wea-
pons, dwellings, agri-
culture, religion and
personal appearance:
do not miss the red feathered head-
dress and ritual pipes. Archeologists deliver lectures in
a small auditorium on the site, and demonstrate the skills of the
Etowah at various times during the year (tel: 404-387-3747 for
specific information). A video presentation is shown on the hour.
The last program begins at 4pm: allow at least 1½ hours to view
the museum and to expolre the mounds, pits, defensive moat and
other earthworks which comprise the site.

Please respect the admonishment not to remove items of historic
significance from the site, and ask about any poisonous plants or
snakes in the area before setting out on a short, self-guided hike
(Tuesday to Saturday 9am–5pm, Sunday 2–5.30pm; adults $1.50,
children $.75). There is a very interesting pamphlet titled
Explorations at Etowah, Georgia: 1954–1956 which explains the
archeological significance of this site. This, plus other books on
Native Americans of the south-eastern United States are available
at the small gift shop.

6. Spa Day

**Back in the city a 'treat yourself well' break with a full or half
day of spa treatments, plus hair-dressing at Van Michael Salon.**

This day can last as long as you choose, but to make the most of it,
I recommend a full or half day, for individuals of either sex, or for
couples, both at Spa Sydell and the Van Michael Salon in Buckhead. If you opt for dinner afterwards, be sure to reserve a table at
Chops (tel: 404-262-2675), and take casually elegant clothing
along to change into. Spa Sydell and the Van Michael Salon will
require reservations as well, so it is best to book ahead quite early
in your Atlanta stay, or even before you arrive in town.

From the Lenox Road/Peachtree Road NE axis, head south down
Peachtree, crossing Piedmont after about a mile. About half a mile
further on turn right on West Paces Ferry Road NW. You will see
a 17-story, green glass high-rise – the Buckhead Plaza Building –
on your left. Turn left at the first light and circle left to valet parking ($1 tip). Ask to be directed to Sydell's. **Spa Sydell** (One Buck-
head Plaza, 3060 Peachtree Road NW, tel: 404-237-2505. Monday
to Thursday 9am–9pm, Friday and Saturday 9am–6pm, Sunday
noon–6pm) is a quiet, serene space in ultra-minimalist peach-tones,
with fresh flowers and touches like (young) director Karen Harris's

grandmother's crocheted throws at the foot of the massage tables. This is a place with world-class calm – much needed in Atlanta, which tends to exhibit so little tranquillity at street level.

There are various programs to choose from: the Day Program lasts 5 hours and includes a facial using Sydell's own natural products, a full hour's body massage, manicure (please note: all instruments are double-sterilized between uses), pedicure, light gourmet lunch and, if you want, an artistic make-up application. The Spa Day adds an extra hour of service – a body treatment involving hydrotherapy or exfoliation, or an herbal wrap. The Deluxe Spa Day adds another hour yet – and another choice of body treatments. (Prices at press time ranged from $44.50 for a manicure and pedicure, to $165 for the Day Program, or $200 for the Spa Day.) Spa Sydell offers all services for both men and women. The staff are all specifically licensed according to their skills, and the majority of them have worked for the family for many years.

Van Michael Salon

After completing your program at Sydell's, flow – you will be *that* relaxed – across the street to Van Michael to get your hair cut and styled and make-up applied. But prepare yourself: the **Van Michael Salon** (39 West Paces Ferry Road, tel: 404-237-4664. Monday 9am–6pm, Tuesday to Friday 8.30am-8.30pm, Saturday 8.30pm–5pm) is going to be like a post-sauna cool dip after serene Sydell's. Van Michael's is all black leather and lace, a futuristic, honky-tonk rock-without-rollers show – with very serious, very precise styling going on simultaneously. High energy, high profile, one of the brother-partners (they hail from Cartersville, Georgia) was named North American Hair Stylist of the Year in 1993. The salon has merited scores of other significant awards but the hairstyling speaks for itself.

It takes a minimum of six weeks to book an appointment with either Van or Michael, but the other 50 stylists and chemical technicians on the staff are hand-picked by the owners. Every client gets a clarifying scalp massage and cleansing treatment with Aveda herbal products

Salon styling

Chops is tops

(no petrochemicals; no animal-tested or animal products), a consultation with a stylist, then a hair cut, blow dry, styling, and free make-up application at the end: no charge for even full evening make-up. Cuts range from $25 to a high of $60.

Chops (see the *Eating Out* section) is next door to Sydell's. It is as frenetic as Van Michael's but in a less avant-garde way: lots of beef, but no leather. And if you are currently off red meat, the seafood's also just over-the-top good, not to mention the wine from their extensive cellars. As this entire day is designed for romantic self-indulgence, why not pull out all the stops and go for a bottle of champagne as well?

7. An Atlanta Shopping Spree

A day of shopping and snacking: Phipps Plaza mall, Lenox Square mall, and high tea at the Ritz-Carlton.

Begin this day of suburban mall shopping with a phone call: make reservations for the last sitting of **Afternoon Tea** at the **Ritz-Carlton Hotel, Buckhead** (3434 Peachtree Road NE, tel: 404-237-2700; in the hotel's Lobby Lounge, 3–5pm). Then, set out for an early breakfast. From the intersection of Lenox Road and Peachtree Road NE, go north on Peachtree, staying in the center lane of traffic, and passing the Phipps Plaza mall – your first stop after breakfast – on your left. Drive on, passing Cherokee Plaza on your right, as well as MARTA's Brookhaven station (right and left). Just over 2 miles from Lenox Road, turn left at **The Original Pancake House** (4330 Peachtree Road NE, tel: 404-237-

Original Pancake House

4116. Monday to Friday 7am–3pm; Saturday and Sunday 7am–4pm). Whatever you order will feature the freshest ingredients, the meats are dry-cured and hickory-smoked, and the batters (like their sour dough, for example) are hand-blended from original recipes.

For a real feast, try the 'Oven-Baked Dutch Baby,' a sort of mega-egg-rich popover served with lemon wedges, whipped butter and powdered sugar; or the apple pancake, also an oven-baked pastry with fresh Granny Smith apple slices and Sikiyian cinnamon. Not for weight watchers, this place!

Backtrack now to **Phipps Plaza**. Stay in the right lane on Peachtree and turn right into Wieuca Road NE, then left into the mall parking lot. If it is especially hot, park on a lower level of the parking garage beside the Lord & Taylor department store. At the information desk, on Level M1, pick up a brochure/plan of the shops, restaurants and cinemas in the mall. Phipps Plaza opened over two decades ago, but was renovated in 1992 to the tune of 140 million dollars, metamorphosing into a dazzling commercial butterfly. Lord & Taylor, Parisian and Saks Fifth Avenue department stores anchor the big tent that every shopping mall really is, but, in between, specialty shops, the food court, cafés, Carter-Barnes Hair Artisans (really a 'day spa') and many others add to the mall's up-market spice.

I especially like **The Civilized Traveller** – travel books, gadgets and gifts – **Tiffany & Co** jewelers (who carry Elsa Peretti, amongst others), Nike Town (for Nike this and that), and **The Discovery Store**, with its gleanings from nature in all her diversity. **A/X Armani Exchange** has casual clothes perfect for Atlanta.

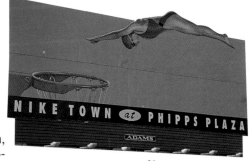

Net gain at Phipps

If it's lunchtime when you get through mall-worshipping, you cannot do better than **The Peasant Uptown**, located on Level M2 (tel: 404-261-6341; Sunday to Thursday 11am–3pm, 5.30–11pm; Friday 11am–3pm, 5.30pm–midnight; Saturday 11am–3.30pm, 5.30pm–midnight). This restaurant is a cool, airy retreat from the rigors of contemporary consumerism. I usually eat at the Colonies-Tropical bar: Oriental grouper filet or an immense salad, maybe follwed by raspberry bruleé. Do not forget, though: you have High Tea ahead of you.

After lunch, make your way back to your car and Peachtree Road again. Turn right and proceed – staying in the left lane – for about 500yds to the Peachtree Road entrance to **Lenox Square** mall (3393 Peachtree Road NE, tels: 404-233-6767 and 800-344-5222). Park near Houlihan's or Rich's, along with Macy's and Neiman Marcus one of the mall's three anchors. Compared to Phipps Plaza, Lenox Square is a behemoth: the largest shopping mall in the southeast. In fact, it is a city: if you're staying at the JW Marriott, you really need never go anywhere else. There are over 200 shops under one roof here, the roster changing a little as Dunhill departs, and The Body Shop comes aboard. **Rich's**, an Atlanta institution since Morris Rich opened his first store in 1867, is a grand old department store with a flash new face. **Nieman Marcus**, the upstart from Texas, is at the top of the department store food-chain. En route between the tent-poles, there are clothing

stores, shoe stores, a chemist's, beauty salons, cinemas, restaurants, and wheeled booths selling such things as 1996 Olympics paraphernalia, if you just have to purchase a **Whatizit** doll – the Olympic mascot. Good choices for women's clothing are The Limited and Ann Taylor. The Gap and Banana Republic are nouveau-casual unisex.

The Metropolitan Museum of Art store features excellent museum copies, cards and books; 'foreigners' such as Crabtree & Evelyn and Laura Ashley are represented as well. If you start suffering from overload, come back another day for shopping, a film, and lunch at Nieman Marcus's Zodiac or at Mick's, an art deco/50s-styled diner. You can have just a slice, or get an entire Oreo Cheesecake to go, made on the premises.

If you're up for yet more shops, head for **Perimeter Mall**. This can be combined with late afternoon coffee or dinner at the elegant **Café Intermezzo** (4505 Ashford Dunwoody Road, Park Place, tel: 404-396-1344. Sunday noon–12.30am, Monday to Thursday 9am–12.30am, Friday 9am–1.30am, Saturday 10am–1.30am). To get there, proceed 4 miles north on Peachtree Road NE/Peachtree Industrial Boulevard. Turn left into Johnson Ferry Road. Bear right into Ashford Dunwoody Road after 2 miles, proceed another mile and signings for Perimeter Mall will appear on your left. From the mall, Park Place and the Café Intermezzo are a stone's throw away, just across the street.

Tea at the Ritz-Carlton

Tea at the **Ritz-Carlton**, Buckhead, across Peachtree Road NE from Lenox Square, is served in the Lobby Lounge, where the Ritz-Carlton Orchestra's conductor William Noll may well be playing the Steinway for your enjoyment. You will have your pick of imported teas, a selection of tea sandwiches, scones with Devonshire-esque cream and strawberries with Grand Marnier and cream. Oh yes – there is champagne by the glass, as well as assorted ports and sherries for weary shoppers. Hats are optional, but it would be appreciated if you dressed up a bit.

Chastain amphitheatre

8. Classic or Country Chastain

If you are planning to visit Atlanta during the months of June, July, or August, this is one evening's entertainment I would try to arrange in advance by faxing to procure tickets. The hotel concierge will probably have an advance program of performers to send you, and you can make your selection – the further in advance of arrival time the better. An evening spent at the al fresco Chastain amphitheatre, with a special picnic dinner prepared by your hotel, is a pleasure to remember. The skies are usually starry and the music is bound to be good.

You may choose a performance in the **Atlanta Symphony's Classic Chastain series**: Ray Charles, The Ramsey Lewis Quintet, Mannheim Steamroller, Natalie Cole, Lou Rawls, or other performers of such stature. You may, on the other hand, prefer to attend something in the **Country Chastain series**: Mary-Chapin Carpenter, Willie Nelson & Family and Emmylou Harris have been recent guests.

It is possible to reserve tables for six, box seats, various terrace levels, or a space on the lawn but, rain or shine, the 8.30pm concerts go on. (Lawn subscribers, asked to bring their own blankets, may wish they had brought their own umbrellas as well.) When the weather is clement, however, these evenings are magical. Atlanta Symphony Season Ticket Office, 1293 Peachtree Street, 4th Floor, across from the High Museum of Art (tel: 404-898-1189, fax: 404-898-9297; Monday to Friday 9am–5pm).

All concerts are held at the **Chastain Park Amphitheatre**, Powers Ferry Road and Stella Drive, tel: 404-231-5888. Representative single ticket prices at the time of going to press: box seats $36.50; center and side terrace seats $32.50; lawn $16.

Drinks and/or dinner at the Sun Dial, the revolving lounge and restaurant atop the Westin Peachtree Plaza Hotel; followed by the Hard Rock Café Atlanta; finish the evening at a trendy club called Velvet.

A few words about this evening. Depending on your age, interests, temperament and ability to sustain noise, you may opt for simply drinks-with-a-view at the rather sedate Sun Dial, or for dinner at the predictably boisterous, young Hard Rock Café Atlanta. Or perhaps the rest of the night at outré 'alternative' Velvet, one of the city's hottest clubs – but perhaps too far out there on the Virginia-Highland/Little-Five-Points fringes-of-gender-blurring for some visitors, if you catch my drift.

Please reserve ahead at the Sun Dial, if you opt for dinner (73rd story, Westin Peachtree Plaza Hotel, 210 Peachtree Street NW, tel: 404-589-7506. Monday to Saturday 11.30am–2.30pm lunch, Sunday 10.30am–2.30pm brunch buffet, Sunday to Thursday 6–10pm dinner, Friday and Saturday 6–11.30pm dinner; drinks, first come first served).

You could and can easily get to the Peachtree Center N1 station by MARTA from the Lenox NE7 station. But you will need to consider how late you will be coming back: you could plan to go downtown by train and return to Lenox by taxi, for safety's sake, or simply because the trains have stopped running.

Marriott Marquis Hotel

From Peachtree Center N1, follow signings for the **Westin Peachtree Plaza** and ascend to street level via three escalators, the second one rather terrifyingly high. You will come out on Peachtree Street, in the heart of downtown, which is almost directly across from Atlanta's Hard Rock Café, a possible dinner spot, or coffee and dessert stop after dinner.

If you have time to spare, wander down to the **Atlanta Marriott Marquis Hotel**, at 265 Peachtree Center Avenue NE, just to have a peek inside the 48-story, 515ft-high atrium with its hanging fabric sculpture – another John Portman and Associates-designed whopper of a skyscraper-cum-hotel, all 1,674 guest rooms of it.

Then, head back along Peachtree Street, where you will cross International Boulevard and enter the lobby of the Westin Peachtree Plaza. The human-scaled lobby and shopping gallery belie the fact that this is the tallest hotel in the United States.

But when you board the glass bubble elevator, which mounts to the top story via a glass-encased tube (elevators will be marked 'For Sun Dial and Lounge'), you will experience a heart-stopping, floor-by-floor ascent, and a matchless panorama of the city and surrounding countryside en route: be sure to pick a clear evening for the best views.

At the top, the **Sun Dial** completes one revolution per hour, and your waiter or waitress can identify the slowly passing parade of downtown skyscrapers, or point out Stone Mountain's massive bulge of granite which lies about 16 miles to the east. The menu's not up to Atlanta's best, but you can't have everything: this is good, solid, if pricey American fare, heavy on beef. And you can't beat the view.

Down below, the **Hard Rock Café Atlanta** (215 Peachtree Street NE, tel: 404-688-7625. Monday to Sunday 11am–1am, bar till 2am) will be familiar to those who've visited the chain's other incarnations worldwide: rock and roll (loud), great burgers, rock iconography ambience, and those T-shirts, plus sundry other Hard Rock Café paraphernalia you may want to take home with you, for a price. I wanted a pink leather jacket, but they were out of them. The place has great, raw energy: who cares about the queue out the door (no reservations).

If you want to investigate **Velvet's** brand of 'subversive entertainment' (89 Park Place, tel: 404-681-9936. Wednesday to Monday 10pm–about 4am), you might give them a call and see what's up for the evening in terms of specially invited clientele/musicians/shows. Suffice to say, this is the band U2's favorite haunt when they're in town. Then, on into the night, or a quick call for a taxi to Buckhead.

EXCURSIONS

1. Chateau Elan

A few hours, or a few days, at a resort-cum-winery located on Atlanta's doorstep.

As they say of **Chateau Elan**, about a half-hour's drive north-east of Buckhead: 'someone finally bottled the perfect resort.' From the beautiful, unabashedly ersatz 16th-century chateau, which houses the Hospitality Center and **winery** proper; to the plush 150-room Inn at Chateau Elan; to the handiwork of Georgia's premier vintner, Brad Hansen, the par-71, 18-hole championship Chateau Elan **Golf Course**, and the **Spa** at Chateau Elan – everything here from

Chateau Elan

sports massage to something called an herbal wrap package – this venue is something else entirely for 'The Peach State,' How long a visit you schedule is entirely up to you.

Drive up from Atlanta for a tour of the winery and a wine tasting (winery tours operate Monday to Friday, on the hour, 11am–4pm; Saturday and Sunday, on the half hour, 11am–5pm), book treatments at the Spa at Chateau Elan (tel: 404-867-8746, toll free 800-233-9463), plan a week or weekend,

with or without golf, at the Inn (tel: 404-441-9463, toll free 800-233-WINE), or come for the golf alone (tel: 404-339-9838). Take I-85 north-east out of Atlanta. Approximately 30 miles beyond the Perimeter exit I-85 at Exit 48 into Route 211, following signings for Chateau Elan.

The winery's **Spirit of France Celebration**, held annually the weekend prior to Bastille Day (July 14) is a great time to plan a visit. Juried art shows, hot air balloon rides, helicopter tours, special menus created by Corporate Executive Master Chef, Bernard Groupy and, of course, **Concerts in the Vineyards** (you sit on a

Wine tasting with Elan

blanket sipping a little or a lot of Chateau Elan's award-winning vintages) make this two-day festival worth planning ahead for. Write Chateau Elan, 7000 Old Winder Highway, Braselton, Georgia, 30517. Call 800-233-WINE or fax 404-867-8714; double occupancy at the Inn: $99–$149. Do not miss the Wine Market and Gift Shop at the Hospitality Center, where gourmet foods like honey, preserves, mustards, crackers and cheeses, plus Chateau Elan's Summer Wine, Cabernet Sauvignon and Sauvignon Blanc, Chardonnay and Riesling wines are all on sale.

2. Monastery of the Holy Ghost, Conyers

A short visit or a scheduled retreat at a Trappist Monastery (couples are welcome).

For the Cistercians of the Strict Observance, an order of Catholic monks founded in the 11th century to reform the Benedictines, greater simplicity was a stated goal. Further reformed in the 17th century by a movement originating at the monastery of La Trappe, the community at Conyers, Georgia's **Monastery of the Holy Ghost** is part of the contemplative order of Cistercians who are known today as the Trappists.

These men, who lead a life of 'hidden fruitfulness' involving prayer, manual labor and spiritual reading, believe the monastery, and their life in and around it, constitutes a 'school of love,' states Guestmaster Father Alberic. What they are schooled in here is learning how to love – no less, no more. Following three vows (of Stability, Obedience and a Conversion of Manners), their goal is to learn to live out their lives loving a chosen group, their Trappist brethren. What Father Alberic feels a retreat can offer visitors is a direct experience of the 'utterly fortuitous nature of God's love,' an experience of grace. He invites

Guestmaster Father Alberic

Monastery church

guests to 'come aside a while,' to step briefly out of their hectic daily existence and be silent; to experience the peace and prayer of this community.

The 50-odd monks at Conyers came here in 1944, when the monastery was founded, but the buildings themselves were not completed till the early 1960s. In the early years, the monks farmed the 1,300 acres, but have since given up farming as unprofitable. Monks such as Father Methodius, who created the stained glass windows in the church, and Father Paul, who is in charge of the greenhouse, and the nurturer of exquisite bonsai, are examples of brethren whose special talents have been encouraged while they continue to support and be supported by the contemplative, shared life of the monastery.

Individuals, couples and small groups of all religious backgrounds are welcome for informal retreats, and are asked to donate according to their means: there is no established fee. Retreats are normally scheduled for Monday after 1pm to Thursday 1pm, or for Friday after 1pm to Sunday 1pm. There is a set Retreat House schedule, and guests are invited to attend the Liturgy of the Hours, as celebrated by the monks in the monastery church. Anyone who is interested in a retreat should contact the guestmaster well in advance of their planned visit by writing or phoning the Monastery of the Holy Spirit, 2625 Highway 212 SW, Conyers, Georgia, 30208-4044, tel: 404-760-0959.

Take I-85 north-east out of Atlanta. At 'Spaghetti Junction,' take I-285 toward Macon, exiting onto I-20 East for Augusta after 12½ miles. Drive for another 16 miles, to Exit 42. Turn right into Route 20 and proceed past McDonald's, where the road forks. Bear right on Route 138 West. After a further 4½ miles turn left into SR 212, following signings for the monastery, turning left up an avenue of magnolia trees after a couple more miles or so.

Be sure to visit the monastery's book and gift shop, which carries such titles as Father Merton's *Seeds of Contemplation*, along with bread baked at the monastery. Do not miss Father Paul's greenhouse, nor his graceful bonsai.

Father Paul's greenhouse

3. Highlands, North Carolina

A scenic drive north-east of Atlanta, through the north Georgia and North Carolina mountains to the mountain resort of Highlands, North Carolina.

You should allow approximately three hours for your journey by rental car: rush hour driving or weekend driving will be slower. Good maps for Georgia and North and South Carolina are a must. If you are departing Atlanta from Buckhead, proceed in a south-easterly direction down Lenox Road towards I-85. Head north-east on I-85, following signings for Greenville, South Carolina. In approximately 8 miles, you will pass I-285, the 'Perimeter.'

Continue for 17 miles, turning off at Exit 45, following signings for Gainesville, Georgia. In approximately 30 miles, I-985 becomes US Federal Route 23. Continue on Route 23, turning left into Route 441 after 21 miles, all the while following signings for Demorest, Clarksville and Hollywood, Georgia, which you will reach after 11 miles.

Following signings for Clayton (23 miles) and Mountain City (3 miles), go on to Dillard (4 miles), turning into Route 246/106 in Dillard, following signings for Highlands, North Carolina, which is another 15 miles to the north-east.

It is best to make reservations for accommodation in **Highlands** well in advance, as this is a popular mountain resort town, especially busy in spring, summer and fall, when visitors – primarily Americans from neighboring states – drive up to view the flowering shrubs (dogwood, japonica, paulownia and rhododendron, April to May), escape the intense summer heat of the lowlands and, in autumn, to view the drama of the changing leaves. (In summer the permanent winter population of 2,000 swells to some 20,000.)

Call **The Old Edwards Inn** (PO Box 1178, Highlands, North Carolina, 28741, tel: 704-526-5036; open April to November) to reserve rooms in this gracious, late 19th-century lodge, and be sure to make dinner reservations simultaneously at the **Central House Restaurant**, its rustically elegant dining room a favorite of regularly returning visitors who come here for the freshwater fish, the immense, fresh salads, rich desserts and attentive service.

Highlands itself was established as a town only in 1879, but the area is rich in local folklore. Much earlier, the region was discovered, first by the Cherokee Indians and later, by the Spanish explorer Hernando DeSoto. Over the years, well-connected families from New Orleans, Charlotte and Atlanta began to forsake the humid summers of their cities, and flocked to North Carolina's temperate climes.

But the area was only truly established when two developers of Western frontier towns, Clinton Hutchinson and Samuel Kelsey, began to take an interest in

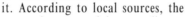

it. According to local sources, the men took a map and drew two lines: one from Chicago to Savannah, and another from New York to New Orleans. The point where the two lines met had everything the developers were looking for: beautiful mountains, fresh air, and easy access from major metropolises. They promoted the area with skill and considerable finance, and Highlands has never looked back since.

From Atlanta, you may also want to phone or write the **Highlands Chamber of Commerce** (PO Box 404, Highlands, North Carolina, 28741, tel: 704-526-2112) for a schedule of cultural events and recreational activities. The **Highlands Playhouse** performances and the **Highlands Chamber Music Festival** are only two of the highlights of this popular summer season.

Opportunities for golf, fishing, horseback riding, tennis, swimming, hiking and white water rafting down the Nantahala and Chatooga rivers are also abundant in and around Highlands. Stop in at the Visitors' Information Center, at the corner of North Fourth and Oak streets, or at the **Highland Hiker** (100 East Main Street, Highlands, North Carolina, 28741, tel: 704-526-5298; open year round) for further information.

The drive up to Highlands through the north Georgia and North Carolina mountains, the scenic drives in the area around the town – located in the **Nantahala National Forest** – falls, such as the misleadingly named **Dry Falls**, and visions such as **Whiteside Mountain** (4,830ft), would be more than enough of a draw for visitors, but Highlands is also a shopper's paradise.

My own favorites among the scores of fine, southern-resort-town boutiques selling antiques, clothing and collectibles are **The Stone Lantern** (PO Box 309, Highlands, North Carolina, 28741, tel: 704-526-2769; open year round), a trove of Far Eastern trinkets and treasures such as priceless goblets and red lacquer chests; and **Southern Hands** (PO Box 1478, Highlands, North Carolina, 28741, tel: 704-526-4807; opening hours vary seasonally), a cornucopia of mountain and southern crafts, including hand-blown glass, woven goods, furniture and carvings.

A couple of mountain folk

Shopping

It is undeniably true that the entire South comes to Atlanta to shop. Whether it is retailers in a four- or five-state circumference coming to bi-annual shows at the big merchandise and apparel marts in order to stock their stores back in smaller-town Dixie; brides shopping in exclusive mall boutiques for their trousseaux (and grooms for their brides' diamonds); high school and college students grazing in the malls every summer for back-to-school clothing; affluent homeowners cruising the Bennett Street antique shops, or alternate-lifestylers rummaging in Virginia-Highland specialty shops and Little Five Points nooks and crannies for futons, planter-sized crystals or naif art, Atlanta is a mecca for consumers.

Sweet Georgia onions

The places to start, if you are here for two days or two weeks, are the malls: Lenox Square, Phipps Plaza, Perimeter and The Galleria, among others. More specific suggestions are sprinkled liberally throughout the *Itineraries* section, and museum gift shops, such as those at the High Museum of Art or Fernbank, are also good places to begin. Here is a primer for novices in the Olympic shop-till-you-drop event – sure to be right up there with the Marathon in terms of attendance, if any Atlantans or their friends are involved.

By the way, what you cannot *buy* in Atlanta (because here it's free), but you might want to subscribe to, before or after your trip, is *Creative Loafing*: $48 per annum. Write The Subscription Department, *Creative Loafing*, PO Box 54223, Atlanta, GA 30308. Pick up a copy of this weekly 'freebie,' which covers everything that's happening in the city, at Oxford Books and elsewhere.

Buckhead

If you're staying in Buckhead, there's a wealth of shops on your doorstep, more or less, though none within safe walking distance of the hotels listed in this guide. Across from **Turtle's** and **Rhythm and Views** (2099 Peachtree Road, NE; tel: 404-606-7131), the music and video superstore, is a glorified warren of shops and small galleries called **Bennett Street**. This upmarket alleyway is home to some of Atlanta's finest antique, home accessory and art dealers. Stop in at **Out of the Woods** and the **Folk Art Imports Gallery** for international, tribal and folk arts – all well represented.

Beaman Antiques, **Nottingham Antiques** and **Bittersweet Antiques** (among other shops) carry English furnishings, antique reproductions and imported accessories, respectively. Carpets and kilims are also available on Bennett Street, though **Afghanistan Nomadic Rugs** (3219 Cains Hill Place NW; tel:404-261-7259) has a more extensive collection, plus jewelry and ceramics.

The **Oxford Bookstore** has two 'generally Buckhead' locations: one at Peachtree Battle (2345 Peachtree Road, NE; tel: 404-364-2700); the other in Buckhead proper (360 Pharr Road, NE; 404-262-3333). **Oxford Too Books**, the location for used, remaindered and art books and magazines is at

Snooty Hooty at Lenox Square

2395 Peachtree Road, NE; tel: 404-262-3411. Looking for an all-night supermarket where you can feast on Georgia peaches (or Vidalia, Georgia's sweet onions)? Try the **Kroger** supermarket, located at 3330 Piedmont Road, NE; tel: 404-237-8022.

Malls

The malls, increasingly, are where Atlantans shop. Convenient, climate-controlled, safe, automobile-friendly, these commercial behemoths dot and blot Atlanta's urban and suburban landscape. Visitors staying in Buckhead will be most interested in shopping at **Lenox Square**, **Phipps Plaza** and **Perimeter Mall** (see *Pick & Mix 7*) as well as **Underground Atlanta**, downtown Atlanta's entertainment and shopping complex (see *Day 1*) – a mall by any other name. At Lenox Square, be sure to stop in at **Rich's**, the South's premier department store and an Atlanta tradition since 1867. Rich's motto is that anyone dissatisfied with a purchase may return it: no questions asked. And Rich's sales are legendary. **Neiman Marcus** also calls Lenox Square home, as does **Macy's**, but speciality shops connect the great department stores like links in a 24-carat chain. Whether you're looking for an Olympic mascot plush toy, imported pipe tobacco, new heels on the spot, airline tickets, a giant chocolate chip cookie or a fedora, you'll find it at this mall.

Phipps Plaza, across Peachtree Road from Lenox, is a more affluent, stylish sister to Atlanta's mall-of-malls. It makes up in luxury what it lacks in size. At Phipps, you'll find **A/X Armani Exchange**, **Tiffany & Co**, **Jaeger** and **Nike Town**, among a host of other internationally respected retailers. Look for *Insight Guides* galore at **The Civilized Traveller**.

Virginia–Highland

At the intersection of Highland and Virginia avenues is the city's most attractive alternative to mall shopping, the **Virginia–Highland neighborhood** (see *Day 2*). Intimate, lively restaurants, bars, bakeries and dessert-eries are interspersed with boutiques and galleries, making this area an ideal place to shop till you drop (into the nearest well-padded chair). The clientele are young, affluent and 'laid back,' as Atlantans are wont to say. Prices for goods are reasonable and what's on offer is generally original, high quality and cleverly presented: no chance of mall-style sensory overload here.

For women's clothing, try **Mitzi & Romano** (1038 North Highland Avenue; tel: 404-876-7228), where the styles are New York-sophisticated, from cunning costume jewelry to whimsical hats and Betsy Johnson frocks. Across the street are **Bang!** and **Rapture** (1039 North Highland Avenue; tel: 404-873-0444), where men's and women's fashions are a bit more *outré*. For eclectic 'antiques'

Aliya Gallery in Virginia–Highland

and gifts, from 1950s home furnishings and a working lava lamp to boxing nun hand puppets and a still-life layer cake composed of dried clover, don't miss **20th Century** (1044 North Highland Avenue; tel: 404-892-2065), where you'll be astounded by Vic and Deloris' cornucopia of camp and class acts. **Maddix de luxe Florist** (1034 North Highland Avenue; tel: 404-892-9337) is my own personal Virginia–Highland favorite. Candles, designer chocolates, sophisticated greetings cards, art books, garden accessories: it's a mad hatter's delight, just about everything you never imagined you'd be buying all under one zany roof. The **Sidewalk Studio** (996 Virginia Avenue, NE; tel: 404-872-1047) is a little more rational: custom jewelry, ceramics, Cherokee drums and gourd rattles. The key to this collection is whimsy.

Little Five Points

Another shopping hub, **Little Five Points**, ground zero at the convergence of Moreland and Euclid avenues, is not quite as user-friendly as Virginia–Highland: skinheads and other belligerent-looking folk habituate this area after dusk. However, it's one of Atlanta's foremost 'alternative consumption' areas.

You won't want to miss the health food/alternative lifestyle emporium known as **Sevananda Natural Foods Community Owned Grocery** (1111 Euclid Avenue, NE; tel: 404-681-2831) or the retro (spective) clothing and accessory shop called **The Junkman's Daughter** (1130 Euclid Avenue, NE; tel: 404-577-3188). Little Five Points has an attitude, but also an edge you won't find elsewhere in the city. Also, it's the place to go for vintage threads, crystals, New Age book, lesbian literature (at **Charis**), and other exotica, or staples of life, depending on your point of view.

Sevananda Natural Foods

But no matter where you shop in Atlanta, no matter what your heart desires, please do not leave town without a Braves baseball cap, a copy of Margaret Mitchell's *Gone With The Wind*, an Olympics T-shirt, and a recording by Ray Charles, of Georgia's official state song, 'Georgia On My Mind.' Whatever else you purchase is entirely up to y'all.

Eating Out

If you parachuted into Atlanta a total of 100 times, the odds are you would land on a restaurant – and a *good* restaurant – some 98 times out of a hundred. The Big Peach has definitely become home to a generation of ardent foodies in the fast, hungry lane. All those two-person, two-income, two-on-display couples have to eat somewhere, three times a day, and delirious dining is the result: a visitor's dream if you are not on a diet.

The following list is nothing if not idiosyncratic. You should not leave Atlanta without stopping in at **The Varsity** on Spring Street (The World's Largest Drive-in), or that Jimmy-Dean/Ford-Fairlane dream of a diner on Ponce de Leon Avenue, the **Majestic**. I can't allow you to pass up that other paean to junk food, on Ponce de Leon, either: the **Krispy Kreme** donut vendors.

A few of my personal favorites are included in the following list which purports only to be one that will keep body and southern soul together. A selection of other restaurants are detailed in the *Itineraries* section; ethnic eateries galore, many too good to be true, are covered in *Atlanta Magazine* and *Creative Loafing* listings. *Atlanta Magazine* also sponsors a 'Guide Line' for Touch-Tone Phone users. Using a brochure available through your hotel concierge, you may dial a wide variety of Atlanta restaurants to make reservations or request a fax of the menu: tel: 404-688-7788; from outside Georgia, 800-297-FOOD.

Mick's Oreo cheesecake and chocolate cream pie

Up-Market

VENI VIDI VICI
41 14th Street
Tel: 404-875-8424
'Rustic Italian cuisine' in a decidedly theater-district setting. This is a showcase for the work of third-generation, Florentine executive chef Emilio Di-Carlo: 'Antipasti Piccoli' (18 daily specialty starters), handmade pastas, whole roasted lamb and duck, suckling pig with chive-mashed potatoes, among other pleasures.

ANTHONY'S
3109 Piedmont Road NE
Tel: 404-262-7379,
Fax: 404-261-6009
This is surely Atlanta's 'Belle of the Ball,' from your first cocktail on the verandah (a 'Frankly My Dear' in a souvenir glass), through 'Roasts Carved From Our Silver Chariot'. The setting's a 1797 antebellum plantation home, and the service, from valet parking on, is Anglo-Atlantan. Reservations urged.

KAMOGAWA JAPANESE RESTAURANT
Hotel Nikko Atlanta, Lobby Floor,
3300 Peachtree Road
Tel: 404-841-0314

High-style down-home cooking

At the Hotel Nikko, this 'three-peach' jewel is, I hear, Elton John's favorite. Stunningly authentic Japanese cuisine in four unique settings: the sushi bar; at white-linen-draped tables overlooking the Nikko's splendid Japanese garden; at the *teppanyaki* grill; or in private *tatami* rooms. Green tea ice-cream, anyone? Reservations urged.

CHOPS
One Buckhead Plaza,
3060 Peachtree Road NW, Suite 150
Tel: 404-262-2675
Did anyone mention the word 'steakhouse'? Thought not. This is a beef emporium of the first order. Featuring aged prime beef and seafood, the menu's ultra-American and nothing but the best, from Long Island Blue Point Oysters, through Large Live Maine Lobsters or Chops Porterhouse For Two, and on to the Fresh Raspberry Tart.

Affordable

BUCKHEAD DINER
3073 Piedmont Road
(at East Paces Ferry Road)
Tel: 404-262-3336
Would you understand if I said that if Anthony's represents 'The Old

South,' this diner represents 'The New South?' Enjoy the glorified pizza, hamburgers, soft shell crabs, onion rings and tarted-up southern icons such as Banana Cream Pie. It's all 'down home' – if home had a pair of BMWs parked out back.

Kahlua Cheesecake

(from The Public House)

INGREDIENTS:
- 4oz butter
- 2C Graham Cracker crumbs
- 3lbs cream cheese
- 3C sugar
- ¼C cocoa
- 6 extra large eggs
- ¼C Kahlua
- ½C per portion cream
- ½tsp per portion chocolate shavings

1. Line bottom of a 10" x 3" cheesecake pan (not springform) with parchment paper. Heat oven to 350°F.
2. Melt butter and combine with cracker crumbs.
3. Pat into prepared pan and bake for 10 minutes. Remove from oven and set aside. Beat cream cheese in mixer till soft.
4. Sift sugar and cocoa together. Add to cream cheese and beat till no lumps of cheese remain. Scrape bowl often.
5. Add eggs and Kahlua.
6. Pour batter into pan.
7. Place pan into a roasting pan filled with 1" of water. Bake the cake in this bath for 3 hours. Refrigerate overnight.
8. To remove cake from pan, dip pan for 15 seconds in larger pan filled with hot water. Invert onto large dish and rap gently till cake slides out. Invert, right side up, on serving dish.
9. Top each portion with whipped cream and chocolate shavings.

One 10" cake serves 10 people.

DANTÉ'S DOWN THE HATCH

3380 Peachtree Road NE, Buckhead
Tel: 404-266-1600
86 Lower Alabama Street,
Underground Atlanta
Tel: 404-577-1800

Twenty-three years in Atlanta, Danté Stephensen's fine fondue cuisine, 18th-century-sailing-vessel décor, live jazz (and live crocodiles in the moat) have been turning heads and returning patrons such as Jimmy and Rosalyn Carter, Burt Reynolds and William Buckley. Reservations urged at both locations.

PEASANT UPTOWN

3350 Peachtree Road NE, Buckhead,
in Phipps Plaza
Tel: 404-261-6341

This mall-side member of the excellent Peasant group looks like the verandah of a colonial plantation – with piano music, a cool, laid-back atmosphere, and scrumptious filets of beef or fish.

THE PUBLIC HOUSE

605 South Atlanta Street, Roswell
Tel: 404-992-4646

Another 'Peasant,' but with a difference. Located in the heart of historic Roswell, in an early 19th-century Victorian storefront, this restaurant features charming décor, Peasant-chain-class service (impeccable), and this author's favorite dessert, bar none, the world over: Kahlua Cheesecake. Peach Pecan Rack of Lamb or Lump Crab Cakes first, though.

Very Reasonable

MICK'S

Lenox Square Mall
Tel: 404-262-6425

This neo-50s-style chainlet of 'diners' has nine locations in the city. Hamburgers, super salads and pasta prevail, plus killer Oreo Cheesecake.

GOLDBERG AND SON, INC
BAGEL BAKERY-DELICATESSEN
4383 Roswell Road NE
Tel: 404-256-3751
Since 1972, the Goldbergs have been serving up award-winning bagels and bialys baked on the premises, as well as Kosher hot dogs, Reuben and pastrami sandwiches. South of New York City, this is the best deli around. Heading for a concert at Chastain? This is a good place to pick up your tailor-made picnic.

Ten types of bagels

ROCKY'S BRICK OVEN PIZZERIA
1770 Peachtree Street
Tel: 404-876-1111
Look, it's a pizza joint. But it's a great pizza joint. Wood-fired-brick-oven baked pizzas, calzones, antipasta and salads – everything you'd expect. Fun, young, and 50 years of getting it right.

THE MAJESTIC FOOD SHOP
1031 Ponce de Leon Avenue
Tel: 404-875-0276
The 'diner at the end of the world.' By all means come here for the sensory overload of Americana, and eat what you will.

R THOMAS DELUXE GRILL
1812 Peachtree Road
Tel: 404-872-2942
This patio-style restaurant with the spray-painted Statue of Liberty out front has been in business eight years,

Tex-Mex, round the clock

and is open round the clock. Noted for its Tex-Mex cuisine, design-it-yourself omelets, chicken burgers, dessert bar, fresh juice bar – and everyone dropping in when everything else is closed.

KRISPY KREME (DOUGHNUTS)
295 Ponce de Leon Avenue
Tel: 404-876-7307
Creative Loafing's Cliff Bostock phrases it best: 'Swill coffee and eat 'em so hot they're semi-solid with cops, the homeless, hookers, yuppies and make-believe leather boys from the Eagle.

ORIGINAL HOUSE OF PANCAKES
4330 Peachtree Road NE
(and other locations)
Tel: 404-237-4116
Please do not confuse this restaurant chainlet with the 'other' pancake house chain: there's no comparison. The concept of pancake batters featuring sour dough, mixed by hand using premium ingredients, was born in 1953 in Portland, Oregon: the idea, and actuality, live on in Atlanta. Try their Apple Pancake, Sourdough French Toast or Dutch Baby and loosen your belt.

Nightlife

Open the 'Living' section of Saturday's the *Atlanta Constitution*, the 'Arts,' 'Happenings' and 'Big Picture' sections of the weekly 'freebie' newspaper, *Creative Loafing*, or the 'Calendar Of Events' chapter of *Atlanta Now*, published by the Atlanta Convention and Visitors' Bureau, and you will see immediately why just about every Southerner under the age of 40 wants to live in Atlanta, or at least close enough to the city to take advantage of the variety of entertainment the city attracts.

Classical and pop music concerts, art exhibits, ballet, dance and theater performances, festivals, performance artists, stand-up comedy acts, film openings, landmark sporting events – there is so much going on in Atlanta on any given evening that it is almost impossible to stay abreast of the listings, let alone attend most of the major shows and games.

A guide of this size can point you in the right direction (the above-mentioned publications, for a start, then the Woodruff Arts Center, The Fox Theatre, The Georgia Dome, the Omni, The Alliance Theatre, Chastain Park, the Coca-Cola Lakewood Amphitheatre, etc), but individual interests and tastes will dictate whether you find an evening spent with wild and wacky Georgia Renaissance Festival devotees, all done up in 16th-century gear, more edifying than, say, an evening down at the Roxy, in Buckhead, listening to Leonard Cohen, or over at the Center For Puppetry Arts, watching *Aesop's Tortoise & The Hare & Other Fables*.

Here is an annotated and selective list of clubs and dance venues you might choose to visit during your stay. For major concerts, night sporting events and ballet, symphony and theater performances, your hotel concierge is your best source of up-to-date information on venues and tickets.

The fabulous Fox

'ELVET
'9 Park Place, Downtown
'el: 404-681-9978
)pen Wednesday to Monday 10pm–
' or 4am.
Vhether it's 'Techno Rave,' Miami/
_atin Dance, 'Aphrodite's Nite-Out,'
'r 'Disco Hell' (70s Disco), Velvet's
theme nights' are baroque, gender-
»lurring, and hot. Not for nothing
lid U2 hang out here when in town.

Rupert's Orchestra

RUPERT'S NIGHTCLUB
3330 Piedmont Road NE
Tel: 404-266-9834
)pen Tuesday and Thursday 5.30pm–
2am, Friday 5.30pm–3am, Saturday
3pm–3am.
No jeans, T-shirts and tennis shoes
allowed here. There's a Happy Hour
buffet served Tuesday, Thursday
and Friday 5.30–8pm. This huge
28,000sq ft venue features the 12-
piece Rupert's Orchestra: Top 40
tunes, Big Band tunes, and DJ-hosted
music between the four nightly sets.
There are seven full-service bars and
a taxi rank outside.

BERLIN
5920 Roswell Road NW,
¼-mile outside the Perimeter
Tel: 404-255-4471
)pen Thursday to Saturday 8.30pm–
3 or 4am.
This is a European-style dance club
featuring high energy DJ-hosted dance
music. It's a predominantly straight

club, with a low cover price, a phe-
nomenal sound and lighting system,
three custom-designed pool tables, a
large outdoor deck, a 'bubbling water wall' and glass-enclosed VIP room:
for Yuppies of all stripes.

BACKSTREET ATLANTA
845 Peachtree Street NE
Tel: 404-873-1986
Open weekends 24 hours, weekdays
11am–7am.
A four-level complex serving diverse
tastes: X-rated cabaret shows, hard-
core dance, country and other dance
lessons, talent search nights – you
name it. Cash required; 21 years and
over only.

DAVE'S & BUSTER'S
2215 D & B Drive SE, Marietta
Tel: 404-951-5554
Open Monday to Friday 11am, Saturday and Sunday 11.30am, Sunday
to Thursday till 1am, Friday and
Saturday till 2am.
Throughout 53,000sq ft of fun, just
about everything is happening here: a
full-service restaurant, six bars, pocket
pool and shuffle board tables, just-
for-fun Blackjack and Midway, video
games, virtual reality, live dance
bands, karaoke, and murder mystery
theatre, etc.

AGATHA'S A TASTE OF MYSTERY
693 Peachtree Street NE,
Half block north of Fox Theatre
Tel: 404-875-1610
Open daily 7.30pm, Sun-
day 7pm; show lasts
about 3 hours $36–
$43.75 per guest par-
ticipant.
A dinner theater ven-
ue featuring 'a five-
course dinner with
wine and murder.'
Audience participa-

71

tion is between courses; the emphasis is on comedy and the dress is casual.

THE PUNCH LINE
280 Hilderbrand Drive NE,
Sandy Springs
Tel: 404-252-5233
Open Tuesday, Wednesday and Thursday 8.30pm, Friday 8.30 and 10.45pm, Saturday 8 and 10.30pm, Sunday 8pm, Thursday and Friday shows are non-smokers only.
Live, stand-up comedy at a place where Jay Leno, Robin Williams and Eddie Murphy first hung their hats. Generally, there are three comics performing each night.

DANTÉ'S DOWN THE HATCH
JAZZ NIGHTCLUB
3380 Peachtree Road NE, Buckhead
Tel: 404-266-1600
Since 1981 in Buckhead, jazz in the form of the Paul Mitchell Trio, Tuesday to Sunday; folk music and guitar on Monday night.
86 Lower Alabama Street,
Underground Atlanta
Tel: 404-577-1800
The Brothers Three are preceded by a jazz pianist. Open Monday to Saturday from 4pm; Sunday, 5pm. Dinner is served until late at both locations. Reservations urged.

THE STAR COMMUNITY BAR
437 Moreland Avenue NE
Tel: 404-681-9018
Open Monday to Thursday 4pm–2am, Friday 4pm–3am, Saturday and Sunday 1pm–2am.
Across the street from acoustic-café **Eat Your Vegetables**, this former bank building features laid-back vocal music, rhythm & blues, alternative rock, and considers itself the frontrunner in the 'Redneck Underground' – with such bands as Redneck, Grease Deluxe and The Diggers. It has received awards for best local music and is a cheap, safe place... with meat, says the owner. Order from either The Elvis or The Elvez (Tex-Mex) Menu.

EDDIE'S ATTIC INC RESTAURANT
AND TAVERN
515 North McDonough Street, Decatur
Tel: 404-377-4976
Open daily 4pm–2am.
In downtown Decatur, upstairs on the square, this no-frills venue features tavern fare and beer plus mostly acoustic acts – pop folk or contemporary folk; a young crowd, and a great, down-home atmosphere.

THE MASQUERADE
695 North Avenue NE
Tel: 404-577-8178
Open daily 9pm–3 or 4am.
Death Metal to reggae to alternative rock; this tri-level (Heaven, Purgatory and Hell) dance club features disco and dominatrix nights, live bands in Heaven, pool tables and video games in Purgatory.

MISS KITTY'S SALOON &
DANCEHALL
1038 Franklin Road SE, Marietta
Tel: 404-424-6556
Such things as a tight-fitting-jeans/best-chest-in-the-West/bikini-dance-

Great atmosphere at Eddie's

Saloon dancing at Miss Kitty's

contest occur here, plus karaoke and line-dance contests with cash prizes. This is in addition to 20¢ chicken wings and $1 draught beer some nights. Urban cowboys, belly up to this bar.

CAFE 290
290 Hilderbrand Drive NE,
Sandy Springs
Tel: 404-256-3942
Bar opens at 4pm, restaurant at 6pm; till 2am week nights, 3am weekends. Entertainment starts at 8.30pm.
A 'live jazz restaurant' featuring reasonable steak, seafood, chicken and pasta entrées, and live entertainment seven nights a week. Adjacent is a sports bar and outdoor patio; free parking; no cover.

JOHNNY'S HIDEAWAY
3771 Roswell Road
(Two blocks north of Piedmont Road)
Tel: 404-233-8026
Open Sunday to Friday till 3am, Saturday till 4am.
Popular with an older crowd, Johnny's is an Atlanta institution. The music is big-band, and owner Johnny Esposito is on hand to make sure his guests have a good time. The food is reasonably priced and there are special events staged throughout the year.

BLUES HARBOR
2293B Peachtree Road
Tel: 404-605-0661
Open every night, call for show times. Blues Harbor, formerly in Underground Atlanta, is *the* place to go if you like the Blues. Everyone who is anyone has played here, from Taj Mahal to James Cotton. The move from downtown to the Buckhead area has done little or nothing to diminish the club's appeal.

Heavenly harmonies

Calendar of Special Events

The single best source of information about scheduled and impromptu seasonal events is *Atlanta Now: The Official Visitor Guide of the Atlanta Convention & Visitors Bureau*, published on a bi-monthly basis and available by writing AC&VB, 233 Peachtree Street, Suite 2000, Atlanta, Georgia, 30303; tel: 404-521-6600. For a recent two-month period, the *Guide* listed some 132 scheduled events, which gives you some indication of the wealth of cultural, sporting and civic activity on offer in the city.

JANUARY / FEBRUARY

The post-season collegiate football play-off game known as **The Peach Bowl** is played at The Georgia Dome, scheduled for late in December/early in January. For information about the game and the downtown parade tel: 404-586-8500.

Martin Luther King Jr Week is celebrated the second week in January, commemorating Dr King's January 15 birthday with a host of activities, performances and gatherings culminating in a 'March of Celebration.' Contact The Martin Luther King Jr Center for Nonviolent Social Change for details (tel: 404-524-1956). January 20, Martin Luther King Jr's birthday, is celebrated as a national holiday.

Atlanta's **Mardi Gras Parade** is organized the Friday before Fat Tuesday in February by the Krewe of Phoenix. The cavalcade proceeds through downtown Atlanta to Underground (tel: 404-392-1272).

The **Atlanta Flower Show**, in February/early March annually at the Atlanta Apparel Mart, is a massive exhibition of flower, vegetable and other assorted gardens (tel: 404-220-2115).

MARCH / APRIL

Easter falls in March or April, and non-denominational sunrise services are celebrated annually at Stone Mountain, most dramatically on the summit of the monolith. Call Stone

Balloon fun

Mountain Park for more details (tel: 404-498-5600).

Water-craft and generally anything that floats, skis or swims is featured at the **Atlanta Boat Show**, held early in March (tel: 404-998-9800).

The St Patrick's Day Parade, March 17, begins at the intersection of Peachtree Street and Ralph McGill Boulevard, and winds up at Underground Atlanta. Bands, bagpipes and beer are all featured and the attire is informal, but green. (There is another St Patrick's Day Parade in Buckhead tel: 404-392-1272.)

The **Atlanta Braves** baseball season runs April to October (tel: 404-577-9100 for tickets to games at the Atlanta/Fulton County Stadium).

Atlanta's premier annual event is the **Atlanta Dogwood Festival**, and activities are spread out over a two-week period in April. House tours, sporting and musical events in Piedmont Park and elsewhere, plus house and garden tours throughout the city culminate in a weekend-long lovefest in the park, usually mid-April (tel: 404-952-9151).

The **Atlanta Steeplechase**, featuring the races, but also the antique autos and all of Atlanta dressed as they see fit for such an event, benefits the Atlanta Speech School. Tickets are available for this event, usually held the first Saturday in April, by mail only. Write: Atlanta Steeplechase, 3160 Northside Parkway, Atlanta, GA, 30327.

The **Atlanta Ballet** Spring Season performances are scheduled from March through May at the Atlanta Civic Center, 477 Peachtree Street (tel: 404-873-5811 for information; 892-3303 for tickets).

The last weekend in April is the **Inman Park Spring Festival and Tour of Homes**, a benefit whose proceeds further restoration work in Inman Park, a Victorian residential area established after the Civil War. The weekend schedule includes historic home tours, guided walks, musical events, craft displays and a parade (tel: 404-242-4895).

Georgia's Stone Mountain Park is the site of the **Antebellum Jubilee**, held the first two weekends in April, and features a Civil War encampment, concerts on period instruments, and late 19th-century arts and crafts (tel: 404-498-5702).

For seven weeks, April to June, the **Georgia Renaissance Festival** re-creates a balmy, ersatz 18th-century encampment in Fairburn, Georgia. Craftspeople, 'fools,' minstrels, knights and their ladies, join in the festivities – all dressed in period costume, or a reasonable facsimile thereof (tel: 404-242-4895).

A Taste of Atlanta is held over three days, usually at the CNN Center, to benefit the Kidney Foundation. Atlanta restaurants participate, and strolling diners may sample their variety of edible wares for a fraction of menu-prices. Firework displays and live music accompany your grazing (tel: 404-248-1315).

Antebellum activities

MAY / JUNE

The **Atlanta Storytelling Festival** is sponsored by The Southern Order of Storytellers and the **Atlanta Historical Society**. Contact The Atlanta History Center regarding this May event (tel: 404-261-1837).

The **Atlanta Film and Video Festival** is scheduled for a five-day period in May and features a juried show of independent works. Contact the sponsor: IMAGE Film and Video Center (tel: 404-352-4225).

May's **Bell South Classic** is a major golfing tournament to benefit Egleston Children's Hospital and attended by some 125,000 annually. Well in advance, reserve your tickets (tel: 404-951-8777).

On a Sunday in June, National Gay Pride Month, Atlanta's **Gay Pride Parade** proceeds from the Civic Center to Piedmont Park. (For details tel: 404-662-4533.)

Sponsored by Atlanta's Bureau of Cultural Affairs, the **Atlanta Jazz Festival** is a major event in June, featuring primarily free events – performances by local to internationally known jazz musicians at Grant Park (tel: 404-653-7160).

The **Atlanta Symphony Orchestra's Summer Concert Series** is held June to August at the Chastain Park Amphitheater. For information concerning this series as well as the regular Master Season and other programs, tel:404-892-2414 (box office) 404-898-1182 (administrative offices).

June to August, the **Georgia Shakespeare Festival** is held on the grounds of Oglethorpe University. For *al fresco* performances and other events call the school (tel: 404-264-0020).

JULY / AUGUST

Independence Day events and parades abound in Atlanta on or about July 4. Major events include the **Fantastic Fourth Celebration** at Georgia's Stone Mountain Park (tel: 404-498-5702), **Independence Day at Lenox Square** mall (tel: 404-233-6767), the WSB **Salute 2 America Parade** (tel: 404-897-

Atlanta Jazz Festival

7385) and *the* big event for runners, the **Peachtree Road Race**, run by some 45,000 participants who pound the course from Lenox Square to Piedmont Park (tel: 404-231-9065).

The Atlanta History Center's **Civil War Encampment**, featuring Confederate and Federal living history interpreters in authentic period costume, brings back to life the world of 1860s soldiers and their families (tel: 404-814-4000).

The **National Black Arts Festival** celebrates the skills and talents of African-American artists, even-numbered years only, in August (tel: 404-730-7315).

Buckhead hotels host the **Atlanta International Food and Wine Festival**, which includes wine tastings and seminars, early in August (tel: 404-873-4482).

The **Atlanta Falcons** football season runs from August to December annually. Fans can watch the team playing home games at the soaring Georgia Dome (for tickets, tel: 404-261-5400).

SEPTEMBER / OCTOBER

Around Labor Day, the six-day-long **Montreaux Atlanta International Music Festival** is held in Piedmont Park, and other venues and free concerts feature nationally and internationally known artists (tel: 404-653-7160).

Georgia's Stone Mountain Park hosts September's **Yellow Daisy Festival**, celebrating the blooming of the Confederate Yellow Daisy with a massive outdoor arts and crafts show, flower show, live entertainment and more (tel: 404-498-5702).

The **Arts Festival of Atlanta** is staged in Piedmont Park, a huge outdoor event lasting for nine days in mid-September and attracting some

two million visitors. A multi-media event, featuring art for sale, but also the performing arts in all their diversity as well as food booths and children's events (tel: 404-885-1125).

The **Atlanta Hawks** basketball season lasts October to March, with games played at the Omni Coliseum (tel: 404-681-2100).

The **Atlanta Symphony Orchestra Winter Pops** (tel: 404-892-2414) and the **Atlanta Ballet** perform October to December (tel: 404-873-5011).

October's big draw is the **Scottish Festival and Highland Games**, held at Georgia's Stone Mountain Park, and featuring kilted clans competing in myriad ways, as well as lots of fiddling and sword dancing (tel: 404-634-7402).

Atlanta's Great Miller Lite Chili Cookoff is another October highlight at Stone Mountain, for those with stomachs of iron. Chili, as dished up by competing cook-off teams from all over the South, is the pièce de resistance, of course.

The **Decatur Heritage Festival**, scheduled for early October on Decatur's Courthouse Square features the work of regional craftspeople as well as down-home music (tel: 404-373-1088).

NOVEMBER / DECEMBER

Each November 11 the **Veterans' Day Parade** winds its way from Peachtree and West Peachtree streets to Woodruff Park, complete with all the time-honored American trappings:

floats, marching bands, drill teams and lots of patriotic pomp and circumstance.

On Thanksgiving Day, the **Atlanta Marathon and Half-Marathon** are run, from Lithonia, Georgia to Piedmont Park (contact the Atlanta Track Club; tel: 404-231-9065, for details).

The **Lighting of the Great Tree** is accomplished on Thanksgiving night at Underground Atlanta's Peachtree Fountains (tel: 404-523-2311).

Christmas at Callanwolde, at the Callanwolde Fine Arts Center (980 Briarcliff Road NE; tel: 404-872-5338) is a delight. For two weeks in December, this Tudor-style home fills with specialty shops, carollers, merrymakers – and Santa.

Kilts galore in October

In Roswell, the **Annual Candlelight Tour of Bulloch Hall** treats visitors to a re-enactment of the marriage of Mittie Bulloch to Cornelius Van Schaak Roosevelt, solemnized in 1853. For **Christmas at Bulloch Hall** tel:404-992-1731.

The **Egleston Children's Christmas Parade and Festival of Trees** is a major Atlanta event, staged to benefit Egleston Children's Hospital. Christmas trees are decorated by area artists and donated for auction (tel: 404-325-NOEL); the parade is Atlanta's most sumptuous (tel: 404-264-9348).

PRACTICAL information

By Air

Visitors from abroad whose primary destination is Atlanta may take advantage of direct flights from major European capitals, as well as Tokyo, but be sure to comparison-shop and check fares which route you through New York or Miami. The secret is booking well in advance of your departure – that, and an energetic travel agent who may be able to put together a very attractive package including reduced rates on otherwise expensive accommodation, car rental, and air, rail or coach travel onwards to other destinations in the United States.

Start early and shop around. At present, British Airways, JAL, KLM, Lufthansa, Sabena and Swissair all offer direct flights from their countries of origin to Atlanta, while Delta, whose hub is Atlanta, offers direct service to and from Frankfurt, Hamburg, London, Madrid, Munich and Paris. USAir connects with Frankfurt, London and Paris.

Through New York, Miami, Los Angeles and other US gateway cities, you may want to make use of carriers such as American, America West, Continental, Kiwi, Northwest, TWA, USAir, United and, of course, Delta. Hartsfield International Airport, some 10 miles south of

Plane facts

downtown Atlanta, vies with Chicago's O'Hare for the title of busiest US airport, and though a beautiful structure, its international arrivals and US Customs areas become very congested in peak seasons or whenever Atlanta's turbulent skies cause delays. The baggage claim area bottlenecks into Customs, which further bottlenecks into a minute area where arriving passengers may check their luggage through to connecting flights. Sometimes, getting through is a breeze.

Realistically, from Passport Control to airport shuttle bus, you may well need an hour and a half. Be absolutely candid on your Customs forms, and patient with the US Immigration staff in the Passport Control area: these officials are vigilant guards against those attempting to enter the country illegally and those bringing in drugs – the whole atmosphere may seem paranoic and intense to visitors arriving from an all-but-borderless EC.

Useful Telephone Numbers

Some of the airlines serving Atlanta: American tel: 800-433-7300, America West tel: 800-247-5692, Continental tel: 800-525-0280, Delta tel: 800-221-1212, Kiwi Airline tel: 800-JET-KIWI, Northwest tel: 800-225-2525, TWA tel: 800-221-2000, United tel: 800-241-6522, USAir tel: 800-428-4322. Airport Bus Service: AAA Airport Shuttle tel: 404-934-8003, Atlanta Airport Shuttle tel: 404-524-3400.

Visitor Assistance: Atlanta Convention & Visitors Bureau tel: 404-222-6688. Georgia Department of Industry, Trade & Tourism tel: 404-656-3545. Multi-lingual Visitor Assistance tel: 404-873-9170. **Travelers' Aid:** has one location near the Arrivals Area at Hartsfield airport; this United Way-funded charity assists travelers faced with crises of all sorts: tel: 404-766-4511 or 404-530-9746 (Centrex).

By Road

The Interstate Expressway System connects Atlanta with Chattanooga, Tennesee, via I-75 to the north-west; Charlotte, North Carolina, via I-85 to the north-east; Charleston, South Carolina, via I-20 and I-26, and Savannah, Georgia, via I-75 and I-16, to the south-east; Miami, via I-75 and the Florida Turnpike, to the south; New Orleans, via I-85, I-65, I-12 and I-59, to the south-west; and Birmingham, Alabama, via I-20, to the west. Visitors in a hurry travel the interstates; those who want to experience James Dickey's South, Eudora Welty's South, and Alice Walker's South, take the secondary roads. If you plan to do a lot of traveling à la Kerouac, consider signing on with AAA, the Automobile Association of America, for six months. One of their services is mapping out automobile trips with handy maps, a must for foreign visitors adrift in sign-poor America, especially between, say, Possum Kingdom, South Carolina, and Nankipooh, Georgia, if you catch my drift (tel: 404-843-4500).

Note: rush hours in Atlanta, from 6.30–9am and again from 3.30–7pm can be brutal anywhere within 'the Perimeter,' or ring road, I-285. In bumper-to-bumper traffic, stay calm, signal lane changes well in advance, and make eye contact with any driver you are asking to make way for you. The speed limit on city streets is 25–35mph; 40mph minimum–55mph maximum on metro interstates and highways. Seat belts are required for drivers and front-seat passengers; child restraints required for children under four; belts may be used for children over three. Helmets required for motorcyclists.

By Coach

This is not a mode of transport I advocate, but then I once fell asleep on a Trailways bus en route from Atlanta to Dallas and gave myself an unbelievable black eye knocking against the window latch. Coach travel in the South, in the summer, will slam-dunk you into a certain stratum of Americana, fill your eyes with sun and your stomach with machine-made coffee. If you must, call Greyhound Lines Inc, 81 International Boulevard NW: tel: 404-522-6300.

By Rail

Amtrak, via the trusty *Crescent*, connects Atlanta's 1688 Peachtree Street station with points north and south – for visitors in no hurry to get from Point A to Point Z, with an alphabet of stops in between. Contact Amtrak: Southern Railway's Peachtree or Brookwood stations; 1688 Peachtree Street NW; tel: 800-USA-RAIL.

Georgia on my mind

When to Visit

Whether you come in summer, for the Atlanta Braves baseball season, or in fall and winter, for football or basketball, late spring through early autumn for the Atlanta Opera, or June through August, for the *al fresco* concerts at Chastain Park, Atlanta always has more experiences to offer than you could ever hope to pack into your short stay.

But, if you have a choice, forego just about anything else one year, and come to Atlanta in mid-April for the Atlanta Dogwood Festival – celebrated in Piedmont Park, and throughout the entire city, wherever one of these snowy trees, which are true symbols of the city, bloom. Useful numbers for information on upcoming attractions: tel: 404-222-669, 800-283-6699.

The 1996 Olympics

Eight million tickets for the 1996 Summer Olympic Games in Atlanta, the XXXVI Olympiad, will go on sale in 1995. The events, which are scheduled from Satur-

day, July 20 through to Sunday, August 4, 1996, will be held within The Olympic Ring – an imaginary circle with a radius of 1½ miles, extending from the Georgia World Congress Center through the heart of the city.

Six events will be held at the 3,200-acre Olympic Park at Stone Mountain; yachting events, off the coast of Savannah, Georgia. More information regarding ticketing and availability may be procured by writing the Georgia Department of Industry, Trade and Tourism, PO Box 1776, Atlanta, GA 30301-1776; tel: 404-656-2566, fax: 404-651-9063.

Just about everything you could ever want to know about the State of Georgia is contained in this organization's annual magazine, *Georgia On My Mind*, the official travel guide published jointly with Publication Concepts Inc, 1240 Johnson Ferry Place, Suite E-10, Marietta, GA 30068; tel: 404-578-0778, toll free: 800-875-0778; fax: 404-578-0676. Definitely worth sending away for.

Visas and Passports

Check with your local United States embassy or consulate prior to planning your trip, but according to current law, citizens of Great Britain and Japan require only their passports for entry into the United States. Canadians must show proof of their residence in Canada; Antipodeans, their passports (expiration date six months post-termination of US stay, please) plus a tourist visa.

Other nationals may face long queues and red tape at United States embassies: in most cases, the requirements for tourist visas are straightforward if time-consuming to procure, but often border on the downright insulting. It seems to be the opinion of the United States Immigration and Naturalization Service that everyone applying for tourist visa status harbors visions of jumping ship in America. Patience and forebearance are the keywords – and starting well in advance of your proposed visit.

Vaccinations

Unless your country of origin is experiencing an epidemic, none is currently required. As is prudent when traveling anywhere in the world, carry on your person prescription drugs and corresponding doctors' prescriptions, translated into English.

Customs

Bring no plant or animal products into the United States, full stop. Check with your local US embassy or consulate if in a quandary about furs or reptile-skin clothing. You may import or export up to $10,000 in currency. Greater amounts must be declared at the border. Allowable duty free imports for visitors staying three or more days: 1 liter of wine or spirits; 200 cigarettes, 100 of any but Cuban cigars or 3lbs of tobacco; plus $100 worth of gifts.

Climate

Atlanta has a heavenly, temperate spring season, from April through mid-June. Summer can be hot and humid, sometimes scorching. Autumn, once again, is perfect mid-September through October. Winter snows are rare, but freak blizzards do occur – beautiful but chaotic for a city ill prepared to deal with them.

Tornado alerts are not uncommon in Georgia, or Atlanta, though funnels rarely touch down in the metropolitan area. Monsoon-like rains do occur unpredictably, in summer, however, and visitors should prepare to seek cover when dark cumulus clouds start piling up over the city: take a windbreaker and umbrella along when you set out on a stormy-looking day. For Time and Temperature: tel: 404-936-8550. Weather: tel: 404-762-6151.

Clothing

Natural fabrics mixed with a dollop of synthetic fibers fare best in Atlanta during the humid summer season and often rainy winter. Almost all Buckhead hotels feature valet laundry services, so leave the heavy travel iron at home. When you fax for reservations, ask whether or not you really need to pack that hair dryer.

Atlantans dress quite smartly for dinner, but tend to be very relaxed at play. In the upscale malls, you will see the entire range of American sartorial schizophrenia: Dunwoody housewives in tennis skirts; high school students dressed in hip-hop eccentricity; businessmen in lightweight suits and power ties; those who should know better clad in 'sweats.' Designer labels abound.

For fair-skinned visitors, wide-brimmed hats and dark glasses are in order for the fierce Georgia sunshine – this is your chance to be a real Southern belle. Plan to dress in layers during spring and autumn, when temperatures fluctuate wildly from morning to night. A raincoat with a warm liner is in order for winter; umbrellas are *de rigeur* most of the year, and a windbreaker takes up little room. If you are planning a stay at the Nikko or the Ritz, very dressy evening clothes will come in handy.

Casual clothing for summer afternoons

Electricity

110–115 Volts; 60 cycles; plugs with two flat, vertical prongs. At Phipps Plaza mall, The Civilized Traveller is a good source for converters, transformers and plug adaptors as well as clever, essential appliances.

Time Differences

Georgia is in the Eastern Time Zone and observes Daylight Savings Time (from 2am, first Sunday in April, till 2am last Sunday in October: 'Spring forward one hour; fall back one hour'). Noon in Atlanta=1pm in Caracas; 5pm in London; 6pm in Paris; 7pm in Athens; 8pm in Moscow and Riyadh; 11pm in New Delhi; 1am in Singapore; 3am in Sydney; 3am in Tokyo; 6am in Honolulu; 9am in Los Angeles; 10am in Mexico City and 11am in Chicago.

GETTING ACQUAINTED

The minute you know you are going to be visiting Atlanta, write or call, during business hours, the Atlanta Convention & Visitors Bureau, 233 Peachtree Street, Suite 2000, Atlanta GA 30303; tel: 404-521-6600 or 800-ATLANTA. Request their packet of publications, including a guide to upcoming events and map. My own favorite map is *Gousha FASTMAP Atlanta*, a fold-in-four-sections, laminated wonder published by H M Gousha: it also doubles as a fan!

How Not To Offend

Foreign visitors often comment on how 'friendly and hospitable' Southerners are, Atlantans among them. But all that Good-Ol'-Boy bonhomie and liberal eye contact is a sort of thick veneer: genuine, but covering up a certain invisible guardedness. In urban Atlanta, where there are visible numbers of people living on the street and a lamentable but persistent tension between the diverse ethnic and racial groups who call the city home, you will do well to maintain a certain 'sense of your own space,' if that's not too New Age a way of phrasing it. Atlantans still address one another as 'Sir' or 'M'am' when addressing a stranger, asking for directions, or initiating conversation with a stranger from another stratum, be that stratum delineated by age, race or social standing. When in doubt, observe closely: 'M'am, could you possibly tell me which Peachtree Street, or is that Road, this is?'

Vital Statistics

Population: City of Atlanta 394,017; Metropolitan area 2,959,900 (1990 census). Elevation: 940–1,050ft. Area: Metropolitan area 5,147sq miles; City of Atlanta 131sq miles. Approximate annual rainfall: 50 inches.

MONEY MATTERS

Banks

Located in Lenox Square mall are branches of South Trust Bank, Trust Company Bank, plus NationsBank and Wachovia Automated Teller Machines. There are scores of banks in the Buckhead area. Your best bet is to enquire of your concierge: specify the service you want, and make use of the hotel shuttle if possible.

Credit Cards and Travelers' Checks

Americans use primarily 'plastic' (credit cards) when traveling, and Atlanta is no exception. Most major cards are accepted by most reputable businesses, as are travelers' checks, though the city is still provincial enough to raise an eyebrow at checks drawn on foreign banks. In the event of loss or theft call the following American Express tel: 800-528-4800, AT&T tel: 800-222-0300, Diners Club tel: 800-525-9135, Discover tel: 800 347-2683, MasterCard tel: 800-826-2181, Visa tel: 800-336-8472. For travelers checks: American Express tel: 800-221 7282, Visa tel: 800-227-6811.

Visitors from abroad should purchase dollar travelers' checks in their countries of origin, and plan to charge most of their trip expenses on credit cards. America is not cash-orientated, and foreign currency proves to be a major headache in a land where few banks are well-versed in foreign exchange, exchange bureaux are all but unknown, and rates can be unfavorable. All that said, exchange services in Atlanta can be found at the following addresses: Ruesch International 191 Peachtree Street, Lobby Level tel 404-222-9300; Thomas Cook Foreign Exchange, 245 Peachtree Center Avenue Marquis One Tower, Gallery Level (also at Buckhead) tel: 404-681-9700, toll free: 800-582-4496.

Tipping

Taxis: 15 percent of meter reading. For airport skycaps: $.50–$1 per bag for curb service; more if bags are carried further. Hotel bellpersons: $1 per bag. Hair stylists, barbers: 20 percent of bill. Restaurants: 20 percent is standard.

Taxes

Georgia's statewide sales tax is 4 percent.

GETTING AROUND

For the purposes of a short, happy, stressless stay in Atlanta, I advise planning ahead: book your hotel accommodation well in advance, either from the United States or from abroad and make good use of a travel agent and fax machine; be sure you take at least one current, valid internationally accepted credit card (such as Visa, Mastercard or American Express) and request an adequate credit ceiling for your accommodation, transportation, dining and shopping needs; enquire from your hotelier by fax about hotel-sponsored transport from Hartsfield Interna-

tional Airport; rent a car at your hotel, if possible, or from a hotel nearby, once you reach your destination, using MARTA trains for some of your itineraries, your rental car for others. Atlanta, sprawling, suburban and subject to extremes of weather, is not ideally suited for pedestrian touring, nor are all areas equally safe for travelers unversed in the American urban realities of random crime against the individual.

MARTA, though swift, reliable and clean, will be taking you into areas with which you are unfamiliar. As in any major metropolis, play it much safer on unfamiliar turf and play it even safer, traveling in groups, after dark. Be sure to lock all car doors while traveling, keep parcels out of sight in the locked trunk of your car, observe the speed limit, and keep your seat-belts fastened. Uniformed Metropolitan Atlanta police abound in congested areas.

Rapid Rail/Bus

MARTA (Metropolitan Rapid Transit Authority) is a rapid-rail system comprising north–south and east–west lines which intersect at the main Five Points station in downtown Atlanta. Stations are designated N, S, E, W or P, denoting their compass relationship to Five Points, P standing for the currently one-station Proctor Creek Line. The Hartsfield International Airport station is designated Airport S7; at present, the station closest to Buckhead is Lenox N7. Schedules are available at all stations; for Subway and Bus Schedule Information, call 404-848-

4711; Airport Service, tel: 404-848-3454; General Information, tel: 404-848-5000; Handicapped information, tel: 404-848-3340/848-5440. Transfers are free on MARTA; enquire about rolls of tokens, weekly and weekend passes, and Transcards, which discount the regular fare. Bus and subway fares payable in tokens, Transcards or exact change.

Atlanta's MARTA buses co-ordinate with the rapid-rail service. The rail system operates from about 5am to about 1am seven days a week, trains running from 8–15 minutes apart. Nearly all stations feature free parking all the time.

Taxis

There are private taxi cab, limousine and even horse-drawn carriage companies in the city too numerous to list. Ask your hotel concierge for assistance or call 404-658-7600 for information regarding taxi companies and fares. Fares at press time: Airport-Buckhead, $25 for one passenger, $13 apiece for two, $9 apiece over two; Airport-downtown, $15 for one passenger, $8 apiece for two, $6 apiece over two; plus 6 percent tax added onto the total fare.

Car Rental

There are numerous car rental companies in the city. It is important to book cars in advance, especially if you want specific makes and models during peak seasons. Check with your travel agent when booking airline tickets to see if there are any special discounts offered you for traveling

MARTA covers the sights

Metropolitan Atlanta Rapid Transit Authority (MARTA)

North Line

N10 Doraville
N9 Chamblee
N8 Brookhaven
Lenox Sq. Mall
N7 Lenox Square
N6 Lindbergh Center
N5 Arts Center
N4 Midtown
N3 North Avenue
N2 Civic Center
Peachtree Center
N1 Peachtree Center
Sweet Auburn Historic District

Stone Mountain

I-285
I-85
I-75
I-20

Proctor Creek Line
P4
Omni/Dome/GWCC
Vine City
Ashby
CNN Center

Bankhead Station

West Line
W5 W4 W3 W2 W1
Hightower
West Lake
Garnett

East Line
E1 E2 E3 E4 E5 E6 E7
Georgia State
King Memorial
Inman Park/Reynoldstown
Edgewood/Candler Park
East Lake
Decatur
Avondale
Zoo/Cyclorama

Five Points

S1 Garnett
S2 West End
West End Historic District
S3 Oakland City
Underground Atlanta
S4 Lakewood/Ft. McPherson
S5 East Point
S6 College Park
Hartsfield Atlanta International Airport
S7 Airport

South Line

N1 Peachtree Center Station
Peachtree Center

N7 Lenox Square
Lenox Square

S2 West End Station
Hammonds House
bus route #67
Wrens Nest
bus route #67
Hammonds House
bus route #71

W1 Omni/Dome/World Congress Center Station
CNN Center
Omni Coliseum
World Congress Center
Georgia Dome

Five Points Station
Underground Atlanta
World of Coca-Cola
Sweet Auburn Historic District
bus route #3
APEX Museum
bus route #3
Zoo Atlanta
bus route #31
Cyclorama
bus route #31

E7 Avondale Station
Stone Mountain
bus route #120

with a specific carrier. Check also whether or not the car rental company you choose requires a credit card booking. If you are flying into Hartsfield International Airport, various car rental firms are located in the main terminal: my recommendation, however, is to rent a car at or near your hotel in Buckhead where there are convenient locations for Hertz (JW Marriott Hotel, 3300 Lenox Road NE; tel: 404-237-2660, toll free: 800-654-3131), and Avis (the Terrace Garden, Buckhead, 3405 Lenox Road NE; tel: 404-530-2700; toll free tel: 800-331-1212).

Note: if you are driving extensively in the US, you may want to look into buying coverage with AAA, the Automobile Association of America, an organization which affords motorists a package of services/benefits (tel: 404-843-4500).

HOURS AND HOLIDAYS

Business Hours

Shop and general business hours: Monday to Friday 9am–5pm, most shops open on Saturday. Most banks: Monday to Friday 9am–4pm, Saturday 9am–1pm. Mall or shopping center shops, including chemists, have later openings and closings. Lenox Square, for example: Monday to Saturday 10am–9.30pm, Sunday 12.30–5.30pm.

Public Holidays

January 1, New Year's Day; January, Third Monday, Martin Luther King Jr's Birthday; February, Third Monday, Washington's Birthday; April 26, Confederate Memorial Day; May, Last Monday, Memorial Day; July 4, Independence Day; Labor Day; October, Second Monday, Columbus Day; November 11, Veterans' Day; Last Thursday in November, Thanksgiving; December 25, Christmas Day.

ACCOMMODATION

The following list reflects my authorial bias for choosing a home-base-away-from-home in Buckhead, as well as for splurging on accommodation in this particular American city. My theory is that visitors come to Atlanta for beauty and pleasure,

Hotel Nikko Atlanta

two qualities not to be had at a motel on the interstate. Rates quoted are for double occupancy, and may not reflect package or other special options available.

$$$ – $150 upwards
  $$ – $100–150
   $ – under $75

THE RITZ-CARLTON

Buckhead 3434 Peachtree Road NE,
Atlanta, GA 30326
Tel: 404-237-2700,
Toll free: 800-241-3333
Fax: 404-239-0078

Massachusetts architects Smallwood, Reynolds, Stewart & Associates have made this 22-story hotel look intimate and welcoming. Adjacent to Phipps Plaza mall, the Ritz lives up to its historic name, from The Dining Room, Atlanta's only AAA Five-Diamond rated restaurant, to the lofty $900-per-night Ritz-Carlton Suite. The 18th- and 19th-century art collection throughout the hotel merits its own self-guided tours-on-cassette, and Afternoon Tea in the Lobby Lounge is an Atlanta 'event.' The luxury rooms feature marble baths, complimentary movies, and terry-cloth bathrobes; there is an indoor 60-ft swimming pool with sundeck and bar, plus an Executive Fitness Center. Ritzy! $$$

HOTEL NIKKO ATLANTA

2964 Peachtree Road NW,
Atlanta, GA 30305
Tel: 404-365-8100,
Toll free: 800-NIKKO-US
Fax: 404-233-5686

The neo-Georgian Nikko features 440 rooms, a health club, sauna and outdoor

pool, the Mediterranean French Cassis and authentic Japanese Kamogawa restaurants, marble bathroooms, private room bars, the Lobby Lounge and Library Bar, and a 9,000-sq ft Japanese garden – a truly grand hotel. Room rates vary, from the 'Simply Nikko' moderately priced rooms to the 'Presidential Suite' at $1000. **$$$**

JW MARRIOTT HOTEL
3300 Lenox Road, Atlanta, GA 30326
Tel: 404-262-3344,
Toll free: 800-228-9290
Fax: 404-262-8603
This is the most conveniently situated Buckhead location for visitors dependent on MARTA, or addicted to shopping: the Marriott connects directly to Lenox Square mall. This ultra-modern high-rise comprises 371 rooms offering cable TV with movie channels, complimentary robes, dedicated modem jacks, etc. **$$$**

SWISSOTEL ATLANTA
3391 Peachtree Road NE,
Atlanta, GA 30326
Tel: 404-365-0065,
Toll free: 800-253-1397
Fax: 404-365-8787
Adjacent to Lenox Square mall is the Swissôtel Atlanta, its white aluminum panelled exterior with black granite 'flying beam' echoing architect Richard Meier's design for the midtown High Museum of Art. Biedermeier-style furniture, black and pink marble bathrooms, a health club, sauna, weight room, lobby

Terrace Garden Inn

and restaurant art collections (Cartier-Bresson well represented), two fine restaurants – Opus and Café Gamay – round out this modern jewel. There are 348 rooms in total. **$$$**

Swissôtel

EMBASSY SUITES HOTEL
3285 Peachtree Road NE,
Atlanta, GA 30305
Tel: 404-261-7733,
Toll free: 800-EMBASSY
Fax: 404-262-0522
This gem may be Buckhead's best-kept secret: it's an ideal venue for families. The concept is simple: all 328 'rooms' are suites comprising a bedroom, of varying sizes, and a sitting room. Galley kitchens, work area, twin TVs, etc – there are two of everything, at least. A complimentary, cooked-to-order, all-you-can-eat breakfast starts your day and two hours of free cocktails end it. And if you are not satisfied, you do not pay. There are indoor and outdoor pools, sauna, steam room, etc – this is no budget venue. Rates are great. **$$**

TERRACE GARDEN INN, BUCKHEAD
3405 Lenox Road NE, Atlanta, GA 30326
Tel: 404-261-9250,
Toll free: 800-241-8260
Fax: 404-848-7301
Southern hospitality is what comes to mind when you check in here. There are 364 newly renovated rooms and suites, a Health & Racquet Center (including an indoor tennis court, two racquet ball courts, swimming pool, sauna, steam room, and a Nautilus weight room), three dining venues – and MARTA and Lenox Square just across the street. But, really, it is the service in this hotel that makes

the difference, especially for foreign visitors. Most expensive, but good value are the rooms on the private Camberley Club floor. (This, by the way, is where my mother and stepfather always stayed in Atlanta.) $$

DAYS HOTEL
3377 Peachtree Road, Atlanta, GA 30326
Tel: 404-264-1111,
Toll free: 800-325-2525
Fax: 404-231-3497
The modest little Days Hotel is being dwarfed by adjacent high-rises, but has cool views of Lenox Square and suburban greenery. There are 300 rooms with in-room cable and HBO films on TV, in-room safes and coffee-makers (but the coffee itself is on you). The Brentwood Café on the lobby level serves breakfast and lunch. Room rates vary, but won't break your pocketbook. $

HEALTH AND EMERGENCIES

Call **911** in all emergencies – accident, personal or fires – and in medical emergencies for paramedical assistance/rescue and transport to city emergency rooms. For referrals: Northern District Dental Society (Monday to Friday 8.30am–5pm; tel: 404-270-1635). Medical Association of Atlanta (Monday to Thursday 9am–4pm, Friday 9am–3pm; tel: 404-881-1714). Fire Department tel: 404-659-5600. 24-hour Pharmacy tel: 404-876-0381. AIDS Info-Line tel: 404-876-9944, toll free: 800-551-2728; 9am–9pm weekdays, 9am–5pm weekends.

Hospitals
Crawford Long Hospital of Emory University, tel: 404-686-4411; Emergency tel: 404-892-4411. Piedmont Hospital, Buckhead, tel: 404-605-5000; Emergency tel: 404-350-2222. Georgia Baptist Medical Center Hospital, tel: 404-653-4000; Emergency tel: 404-653-4136.

Police
State Patrol tel: 404-624-6077. Police tel: 404-658-6600. For all emergency services: tel: **911**.

COMMUNICATIONS AND NEWS

Post
Navy-blue post boxes are located throughout the city. Post offices convenient to Buckhead are: Lenox Square Station, tel: 404-233-3422, 3393 Peachtree Road NE; Northside Finance Unit, tel: 404-233-4457, 575 Pharr Road NE.

Telephones
Pay telephones are located in semi-enclosed booths in malls, on street corners, outside 24-hour convenience stores and petrol stations – everywhere.

Media
The morning the *Atlanta Constitution* and evening *Atlanta Journal* ('Covers Dixie Like The Dew'), and a 'freebie,' *Creative Loafing*, plus glossy, sparkling *Atlanta Magazine* and classy *Georgia Trend: The Magazine of Georgia Business* are good places to begin exploring Atlanta's print media. There are myriad newspapers and journals serving smaller populations in and around the city.

Radio Stations
Classic Rock and NBC News WQXI 790 AM; Country and Western WKHX 101.5 FM; Soft Rock and Roll WPCH 94.9 FM; National Public Radio News and Classical Music WABE 90.1 FM; Soft Rock and Roll WSB 98.5 FM; The News Station WGST 640 AM; All News Station WCNN 680 AM; Alternative Rock From GA State University WRAS 88.5 FM; Contemporary Rock and Roll WKLS 96.1 FM; Jazz and Gospel WCLK 91.9 FM.

Tickets
For Tickets to concerts/events, call Atlantix (tel: 404-455-7141); or Ticketmaster (tel: 404-249-6400). Sports Ticket Information: Atlanta Braves (NL Baseball) tel: 404-577-9100; Atlanta Falcons (NFL Football) tel: 404-261-5400; Atlanta

To the rescue

Atlanta Botanical Gardens

Hawks (NBA basketball) tel: 404-827-3800; Atlanta Knights tel: 404-525-8900; Atlanta Dragway tel: 404-335-2301; Atlanta International Raceway tel: 404-946-4211; Road Atlanta tel: 404-881-8233.

USEFUL INFORMATION

Attractions

Atlanta Botanical Garden, 1345 Piedmont Avenue NE, tel: 404-876-5858 (open Tuesday to Sunday 9am–6pm, till 8pm in summer). Most exciting is the Dorothy Chapman Fuqua Conservatory, which houses rare and endangered plants, but the grounds also include hardwood forests, an ivy collection and stone statuary and pagodas.

SciTrek, The Science and Technology Museum of Atlanta, 395 Piedmont Avenue, tel: 404-522-5500 (Tuesday to Saturday 10am–5pm, Sunday noon–5pm, closed Monday; children under three free) is a far from static, hands-on museum.

SciTrek Museum

Atlanta Cyclorama, located in Grant Park, Georgia and Cherokee avenues, tel: 404-624-1071 (open daily from 9.30am). A century-old cylindrical oil painting and multi-media presentation of the 'Battle of Atlanta'.

Six Flags Over Georgia, 12 miles west of Atlanta, off Interstate Highway 20, or I-20 West, tel: 404-739-3440 (open weekends, spring and fall, daily in summer), features 331 acres of roller coaster and other rides, shows and diverse attractions.

Zoo Atlanta, located in Grant Park, 800 Cherokee Avenue SE, tel: 404-624-5600 (daily 10am–5pm; closed New Year's Day, Martin Luther King Jr's Birthday, Thanksgiving and Christmas) is for animal-lovers in search of exotic fauna.

Jonesboro, Georgia's Stately Oaks Plantation Community, Madison, Georgia's Heritage Hall, and **Newnan-Coweta**'s self-driving tour of antebellum homes are notable for those with more time in the state.

Tours

Good, general, organized tours of the city are offered by Gray Line of Atlanta (tel: 404-767-0594) and Tour Atlanta (tel: 404-851-2549/2550).

Atlanta Preservation Center offers excellent walking tours of Atlanta's historic districts, including Underground Atlanta (tel: 404-876-2040).

Historic Air Tours can give you a bird's eye experience of the city: 1954 Airport Road, Dekalb Peachtree Airport, Chamblee; tel: 404-457-5217. Tours range from 20–50 minutes; $30–$85 per person, and cover either the Capitol district, the entire city, metro landmarks, or Civil War sites.

FURTHER READING

AIA Guide to the Architecture of Atlanta, by I Gournay with photos by P G Beswick, University of Georgia Press, Athens, Georgia, and London, 1993.

Atlanta and Environs: A Chronicle of Its People and Events, by Franklin M Garrett, University of Georgia Press, Athens, Georgia, 1954.

Days in the Life of Atlanta, by N Shavin, Capricorn Corporation and Norman Bloom Enterprises, Atlanta, 1987.

The Legacy of Atlanta: A Short History, by Webb Garrison, Peachtree Publishers Ltd, Atlanta, 1987.

Atlanta Walks: A Guide to Walking, Running, and Bicycling Historic and Scenic Atlanta, written by Ren and Helen Davis, Peachtree Publishers Ltd, Atlanta, 1993.

Index

ACKNOWLEDGMENTS

The author would like to thank journalist Kat Yancey, of the 'Atlantic Constitution' and her mother Eleanor Yancey for southern hospitality to put Scarlett's Aunt Pittypat to shame. Warm thanks also to Lenox Square's Assistant Concierge Manager, Stephen H Moore, and to Ted Ryan and Anne Isenhower of the Atlanta History Center, who aided in this endeavor above and beyond the call of duty.

Photography	**John Sang Yu** *and*
17, 22	**Atlanta History Center**
49T	**Ray Bouley**
56, 57T	**Chateau Elan**
27	**CNN**
59, 60, 61	**Bob Clair**
5	**Zoë Diakon**
41	**Fernbank Museum of Natural History**
26T & B	**Michael I Goldsholl**
23, 63B	**Bill Gornto**
40T	**Greg Greer**
14, 38B	**High Museum of Art**
23, 63B	**Bill Gornto**
49B	**Gary Lyons**
52B	**Ritz-Carlton Buckhead**
87B	**SciTrek**
43	**Stone Mountain Park**
55T	**Westin Peachtree Plaza**
Handwriting	**V.Barl**
Cover Design	**Klaus Geisler**
Cartography	**Lovell Johns**
Production Editor	**Mohammed Dar**

INSIGHT GUIDES

You'll find the colorset number on the spine of each Insight Guide.

INSIGHT *Pocket* GUIDES

• • • • • • • • • • • • •
United States: Houghton Mifflin Company, Boston MA 02108
Tel: (800) 2253362 Fax: (800) 4589501

Canada: Thomas Allen & Son, 390 Steelcase Road East
Markham, Ontario L3R 1G2
Tel: (416) 4759126 Fax: (416) 4756747

Great Britain: GeoCenter UK, Hampshire RG22 4BJ
Tel: (256) 817987 Fax: (256) 817988

Worldwide: Höfer Communications Singapore 2262
Tel: (65) 8612755 Fax: (65) 8616438

66 I was first drawn to the Insight Guides by the excellent "Nepal" volume. I can think of no book which so effectively captures the essence of a country. Out of these pages leaped the Nepal I know – the captivating charm of a people and their culture. I've since discovered and enjoyed the entire Insight Guide Series. Each volume deals with a country or city in the same sensitive depth, which is nowhere more evident than in the superb photography. 99

Sir Edmund Hillary

NOTES